Long-Distance Romance

BARBARA EATON

Long-Distance Romance

Barbara Eaton

ISBN: 978-1-66786-026-8

*To my mother
and the memory of my father*

Acknowledgments

I would like to thank all of the editors who have published my work, as well as the members of Poets & Patrons of Chicagoland and the Illinois State Poetry Society. My friends have helped to make this book possible, especially Caren Sharp, Caroline Johnson, Mardelle Fortier, and Wendy Morris. My greatest debt is to my family.

Charlotte Digregorio's Writer's Blog, Distilled Lives, vols. 1-5, DuPage Arts Life, Ethos, Highland Park Poetry web site, Illinois Statel Poetry Society web site, Li Poetry (Taiwan), The Muse, The Prairie Light Review, Quantum Pulp, Rambunctious Review, weeds, Wilda Morris's Poetry Challenge

Table of Contents

Completing the Circle

The Father/Daughter Dance	2
The Best Gift	4
Kindergarten Drama	5
The Big Yellow Workbook	6
What Comes After Bunny Ears?	8
First Grade: I Surprise My Mother	10
Second Grade Drama	12
Tony	13
The Abraham Lincoln Pencil	14
Pumpkin Patch	16
In the Boat	18
My Sun	19
Love	20
Fifteen	21
Friend	22
The Boats	24
Three	25
First Love	26
The Break-up	27
I am "The Other Woman"	28
Hopeless Romantic	29
Confession	30
Misanthropist	31
Shining Scientist	32
Gossiping Buildings	33
Thirty-five	35

The Grudge Poems

Grudge #1: Jolene   39

Grudge #2: Jolene, Part 2   40

Grudge #3: My Birthday   41

Grudge #4: The Postcard from Paris   42

Grudge #5: My Grandmother   43

Grudge #6: The Affair   44

Grudge #7: The Last Straw   45

I Must Have Loved Him   46

Summer   47

Tangerine Dream   49

Apostrophe to Iced Tea   50

Summer Fruits   51

Last Tango in Paris   52

Heroic Love   53

Forgotten   54

Kirinyaga   55

The Other Dark Lady   57

On Shoveling Snow   58

Flying   60

Respite   61

September 13, 2007, 4:30 P.M.   62

Miraculous   63

The First Spring Without My Father   65

Random Thoughts   68

Christmas   70

Memorial Day   71

I don't want to write about...   72

What She Needs   73

Every Day   74

Yellow Tulips   75

To My Father   76

Taking the Train into the City   77

War Dream   78

Missing My Dad   80

The Language of Flowers   81

My Father's Sunglasses   82

Part I: "Friends"   83

Part II: Traffic   84

The Little Black Dress   85

Fun 101   87

Surprise!   88

You are Already Loved   89

Pink Cupcakes   90

Long-Distance Romance And Further Dreams

True Love in Westmont   93

Long-Distance Romance Swing Dancing

I Saw You Around, Part I   95

I Saw You Around, Part II   97

The Changeling   100

Going to Santa Barbara   102

September: A Substitute Teacher's Love Song   104

October: Halloween   105

November: Thanksgiving   107

December: Charlie Chaplin's The Gold Rush   108

January: Torch Song   109

February: Valentine   111

March: The Visit   112

April: "No Romance"   113

May: Long-Distance   115

No Walk in the Park   116

My Poetic Process   118

Traveling in my Sleep   121

New Scars   123

Bedtime Story   124

At Long Last, Love   125

Further Dreams

Blue Nightmare, Part I   127

Blue Nightmare, Part II   129

Renaissance Hero   130

Dream Weaver   131

R.S.V.P.   132

For Cecy   133

Cinderella Story   134

The White Girl   135

Strange Dream: Love Triangle   136

Further Dreams   138

Dreams of Milk   140

Scrambled   142

Close Your Eyes   143

Ophelia's Dream   145

Child of My Father, Child of My Love   146

The Phoenix and the Turtledove   148

Three Visions from Shakespeare's *Cymbeline*   150

Vision I   150

Vision II: Acting Iachimo   152

Vision III: The Ending   153

I Dream of France   155

Research   156

Last Night   157

Waking   158

Working Girl

To Sylvia   161

The Affair I Only Dreamt About   162

The Three Candles   164

Back to School   166

"Special Paint"   167

"BZZZ"   168

Regrets   169

Two Secret Gardens   170

Missing the Eighties   173

Moving Dreams   175

The Last Dance   176

Ludington, Michigan: A Childhood Memory   177

Kiki and Ed   179

In Her Shoes   181

The Bride   182

The Tornado   184

Part-time Ghosts   186

Good Luck   187

Goodwill   189

"The Quickest Promise Home"   190

Omega   191

Mamma Mia   192

The Other Movie   193

Coming Home   194

Cruise, Part One   196

Cruise, Part Two   197

Wendy's Poems   198

Through the Window   199

A Bargain at the Price   200

Starry, Starry Night   201

The Pet Parade   203

Summer Coming   204

Slipping   205

Silver Skipper of Gostyn   206

Doggy Dream 208

Cats 209

Spring Rain 210

Coffee House 211

Ariel 212

Sonnet 1 after William Shakespeare 213

Sonnet 2 after William Shakespeare 214

Sonnet 30 after William Shakespeare 215

Sonnet 42 after William Shakespeare 216

Sonnet 117 after William Shakespeare 217

To My Shakespeare Professor

How to be a Great Writer: My Foolproof Method 219

To My Chaucer Professor 220

First Memory 223

My Career as a Ballerina 224

"Listen to Me" 225

Patience 228

The Chinese Dragon in my Mind's Eye 229

Seclusion 234

Compassion 237

What I Told Dr. Mahomet 238

Betrayal 243

Timidity 245

"Not Funny," Part I 246

"Not Funny," Part II 247

The Silent Woman 248

Watches 250

A Golden Shovel Poem: a dialogue between Titania and Oberon 251

A Golden Shovel Poem: *Twelfth Night*: Viola and Orsino 252

A Golden Shovel Poem: *As You Like It*: Rosalind,
disguised as Ganymede, to Phebe 253

A Golden Shovel Poem: *Twelfth Night*: Viola, disguised as Cesario 254

A Golden Shovel Poem: from *Antony and Cleopatra*: Cleopatra   255

A Snake Poem: from *A Midsummer Night's Dream*   256

How do I love thee? Part I   257

How do I love thee? Part II   258

The Sunne Rising   259

Psalm   262

Vacation   263

Completing the Circle

The Father/Daughter Dance

I remember pink and white streamers,
white dinner boxes,
girls in pastel dresses
with peppermint ribbons

stiff little candy flamingoes
jewelry box ballerinas
pirouetting from table to table
in shiny black licorice shoes.

Fathers in black suits
with pink boutonnieres
their shifting little girls
sending green glances
to overcast the evening.

I am ashamed now, remembering
that when you helped me
take off my little cape
I noticed your overcoat was getting old.

You smiled and said, "Let's go,"
as we stood in the doorway.

I remember – how can I forget?
the sinking ringside feeling
of walking in,
spotlighted by those grinning green Mars lights.

I checked to see

if your tie was on straight, Dad,
and I hoped you would be
the tallest father there,
unspeakably relieved
that my dress
wasn't by some accident
black
and my shoes, by mistake,
pastel pink –

loving you, Dad,
because your suit
wasn't light blue
with a black boutonniere.

The Best Gift

If there were a Ph.D. in food, my mother would have it.

She has always been interested in food:
collecting recipes,
trying new things.

My dad went along with it all, even Kretschmar's Wheat Germ.

Not all of her experiments were successful,
but some became classics:
the pineapple upside-down cake for Daddy's birthday,
the lamb cake for Easter,
and for Thanksgiving and Christmas,
the huge turkey
with homemade dressing
and homemade cranberries.

But the best gift
was not food, exactly.

The best gift
was good nutrition
and good health.

Kindergarten Drama

Kevin, long and lanky,
a big boy,
cried when his mom left him
on the first day.

The teacher
made him take a nap
on his red and green plastic mat.

I didn't say anything,
but I wanted to cry, too.

The Big Yellow Workbook

I always sat next to the teacher, Mrs. Butz,
not because I liked her,
but because she always passed out
the big yellow workbooks
while we sat on the floor
in a circle.

Each student's name
was written in big letters
in black Magic marker
on the front of the workbook.

Mrs. Butz held up each workbook,
and you had to read your name,
and come and get your book.

I sat next to Mrs. Butz
because I couldn't see
and I didn't want to miss my turn.
I didn't want anyone to know
that I couldn't see.

One day, Mrs. Butz
tossed the yellow workbook
onto the floor in front of her.
"I'm mad at someone," she said.

It just so happened
that on that day
I wasn't sitting next to Mrs. Butz.

That workbook had to be mine,
but I was afraid to go up and see.

I gathered up my courage,
walked up to where Mrs. Butz was sitting,
and casually glanced at the name.

It was Michelle's!

But my secret was out.

What Comes After Bunny Ears?

There was a chart on the wall in the kindergarten room:
Colors, numbers, and tying shoes.

There was a checkmark next to your name
For each task you had mastered.

I knew my colors,
I knew my numbers,
but Daddy and I were still working on tying shoes.

I don't know how it happened, but somehow
there was a check next to my name for tying shoes.

I had a bad feeling about this.

Sure enough, one day Mrs. Butz was berating a fellow kindergartner
who couldn't tie her own shoes.

"Don't you want to be a big girl?
You have to learn to tie your own shoes.
Cluck, cluck.
Barbara knows how to tie her own shoes.
Barbara, show Michelle how to tie her shoes."

Oh, no!
I remember Daddy said something about bunny ears,
so I made bunny ears out of Michelle's shoelaces.

But what comes after bunny ears?
I hoped for a miracle that did not come.
I waited for Mrs. Butz's wrath.

Sure enough, Mrs. Butz exclaimed, "Barbara!
You mean you can't tie your own shoelaces?
Shame on you!"

That was worse than "Cluck, cluck!"

That very night
Mama and Daddy taught me
What comes after bunny ears.

First Grade: I Surprise My Mother

I got up all by myself
and picked out what I was going to wear:
my blue and green plaid skirt and vest
with a white blouse.
Great-Aunt Pearl made the skirt and vest, so it was special.
It was going to be a special day.
I was so proud of myself for keeping a secret.

I ate breakfast – Cap'n Crunch –
just as usual, thought he secret
was in danger of popping out at any minute.

I put on my coat and walked the two blocks
to Seventh Avenue School.
When I got there,
the class was getting ready:
they had their wood blocks,
metal triangles, and wooden flutes.

We assembled in the gym
where folding chairs were set up
for the audience.

I saw my mother
sitting in the last row.

I tapped my baton
on the music stand
and began to direct the orchestra.

My mother
almost fell off her chair.

Second Grade Drama

Ronald punched me in the stomach.
I had a crush on Franklin McKee.

I wouldn't give Ronald the ball at recess
so he punched me in the stomach.
It hurt.
I was in love with Franklin McKee.

Ronald got in big trouble.
The teacher called his parents.
I felt guilty.
I should have just given him the ball.

But boys should never, ever hit girls.

I was so in love with Franklin McKee.

That darned Ronald.
Maybe I shouldn't have teased him with the ball.

Tony

Nobody liked Tony.
When Valentine's Day came around,
nobody gave Tony a valentine.

One day
I happened to follow Tony
out the door after school.

I noticed
he threw his homework paper
into the trashcan
right outside the door.

I also noticed
there was an "F"
on Tony's paper
and I noticed some angry tears.

I had never seen an "F" before in my life.

The next time Valentine's Day came around,
I gave Tony a valentine.

The Abraham Lincoln Pencil

Michelle and I
were having a disagreement
about the pronunciation of a word.

She said, "Waadle,"
And I said "Wawddle."

I knew I was wrong,
I knew I was just being perverse,
but I wanted so badly
to be more sophisticated than Michelle.

Miss Rotsko ended the argument.
She said Michelle was right.

I was so mad
I broke my brand-new Abraham Lincoln pencil
right in half
over my knee.
It was my favorite pencil.

Miss Rotsko was horrified.
She taped the two halves of the pencil back together
with a big piece of masking tape
and handed the pencil back to me.

"Don't you ever do anything like that again,"
she warned sternly.
"Mr. Biddinger will fire me.

Do you want me to get fired?"
I shook my head. "No."

Every time I used my Abraham Lincoln pencil after that,
the big lump of masking tape
reminded me that I had lost my temper
and almost got Miss Rotsko fired.

Pumpkin Patch

We three girls
piled into the light blue DeSoto
with Mom and Dad.
When we got there,
we all piled out
and each chose one pumpkin,
a nice, big, round one.

Then it was time to go.
I ran to the car with my pumpkin.
"Go around to the other side," said Annalisa.
She didn't want to move over and sit on the hump
in the middle of the back seat.

I ran to the other door with my pumpkin.
"Go around," said Patty.
She didn't want to sit on the hump, either.
I stood there with my pumpkin
and watched the DeSoto speed away.

I sat down on my pumpkin
sobbing so hard
I didn't see the car
turn around.

But I did see
Daddy's big, strong arm
reach out of the driver's window.

"Come on," he said.
Daddy opened the door,
scooped me up,
and put me in the front seat
between him and Mama.

I didn't mind the hump.

In the Boat

I want to shelter his head from the cold
in my arms
his hair gently brushing my neck.

I want him beside me
as we ride in the boat
the wind
and the salt spray
in our faces.

My Sun

Soft rain falling
opens the flowers and they bloom.

Tears help tenderness
grow in the soul.

Warm sun
dries the rain gently
and the flowers smile.

You are my sun.

Love

Clouds darken your smile
when I find goodness also
in things that are not yours.

Ah, but you fail to see
the reason
I find happiness in everything
is because the love you gave me
opened my eyes.

Fifteen

It seems we were married long ago
and we've just had a sort of small fight.

You're angry, but you'll come home,
I know, so I wait up,
I've left on the light.

It's getting late, the sky's gone gray,
but you'll be home soon
and I know what to say.

I love you and you love me
and everything's okay.

But I'm only fifteen, just a girl.
I can't sleep at night in my bed.
I see you, making golden French fries,
dreams of more gentle girls in your head.

Friend

How shall I remember you?
Just a blond young man
in an honest white shirt
with a certain sweetness of spirit.

I was in love with your brother
and you were only a young boy
who played the piano extraordinarily well.

Yesterday
I read that you were gone. "Suddenly,
in an auto accident," the paper read.

The article mentioned
where you went to school,
where you worked and went to church,
even that you played the piano very well.

But the paper didn't mention
how kind you could be
or how kind you were to me
one special time.

We both worked in the same restaurant.
You were a busboy, and I was a waitress.
I stopped by in the steamy dishroom to say hello
and in between racks of cloudy glasses
you told me
your brother was getting married.

When you saw my stricken look,
you spoke
In a voice that gently touched --
I felt more tenderness
than pain --
"Did I say something wrong?
Oh, maybe I shouldn't have told you...."

"Your brother and I were just friends,"
I quickly lied,
"and that was a long time ago."

I'm glad you told me.
You were much kinder to me
than your brother was.

The Boats

The boats adrift beyond the buoys
are silent. Through the soft gray mist
towards the tide, the sea-moss moves.
The blue night's moon shines softly
and the boats are still.

Three

sixpence, love, I whispered.
sixpence
until the snow comes on the windowpane
in the morning, darling, sixpence
and he said maybe, no, maybe.

*

I don't know how the cold winds come
but they blow through the trees
and I should go.
You never should have given me
those memories –
they keep me near
when you would have me go.

*

I take my worlds
and yours
painting them in the watercolors
of my books and memories.
The colors run and aren't true;
I am sorry to put you in my poems.

First Love

Wherever you are,
I am thinking of you
and I hope I will see you again,

When the sky is blue
and the grass is green
and the flowers are coming up
out of the ground.

I will be happy, then,
and you will be kind
but it will be too late
and nothing will be the same.

The Break-up

I felt like I was your shaving cream
all white, like marshmallow fluff
till you took your sharpened razor
and cleanly shove me off.

I am "The Other Woman"

Sometimes
I think of you
and how I may be hurting you
and those you love
and I want to go with the rain
I want to run
and let the wind hit me
and run and run and run.

Hopeless Romantic

I am the most romantic person in the world,
but I have never been in love.

I have often been in love, but I have
never married.

I was almost married once,
but I don't think I will ever marry.

I can't live
without the impending promise.

Confession

Sometimes
the bitch
in me
is easy to find.

But then,
some people
always
know where to look.

Misanthropist

Every time I find
a perfect wall
it has a
damned door.

Shining Scientist

Your world made of glass
filled with metal cages
and confusing mazes
lit with bright
fluorescent light –

Why couldn't I see the love
right there among the Petri dishes
and bacillus-filled tubes –

How could I be so blind
so deaf and dumb
playing with people
and think I could love?

Gossiping Buildings

Let me tell you about myself.
I am McDonald's East in Downers Grove
on Ogden Avenue.

The face I present to the world is new.
I look like a little red brick house.
My interior is stylish and comfortable.
The booths are upholstered in maroon and gold,
and the walls are covered with modern art.

But it wasn't always this way.
In my youth,
I was just a carry-out restaurant.
Golden arches and a little vestibule.
That was about all.
I was made of white ceramic tile.
No air-conditioning.
An electric bug killer.

I remember one blond young man in particular.
He cooked the hamburgers on the grill.
As I said, there was no a/c.
His girlfriend worked at the Stop-'n-Chat in Westmont.
She used to bring him mint ice cream.
I guess it was a love story.
But enough of the past.

Now
there is a middle-aged woman
who comes in every night

and orders two cheeseburgers,
a medium Coke,
and a hot fudge sundae.
She sits alone at a booth
and writes in her notebook.
If only I could tell her what I've seen!

She seems to be wrapped up in herself
oblivious of her surroundings.

The Fannie May candy store
tells me she hangs out there, too.

The same blond young man
used to wash their floors.

Even his old house
on Washington Avenue
tells me
she still drives by.

What is she writing?

Thirty-five years ago,
the front porch of her house
told me,
when he said "Good-bye,"
he added, "I will always love you."

Thirty-five

I let him go
without a fuss.

I heard
he married Junie Moon.

I promised myself
I would look him up
when I was thirty-five.

I would walk right into his laboratory
wherever he was.

I would be so beautiful
and smart and successful
that I would win him back.

When I was thirty-five.

     * * *

As it turned out,
I didn't have to wait
until I was thirty-five.

He transferred to the U of I where I was attending
two years later.

We ran into each other
He asked me how my plans were progressing,
and I asked him about his plans.

He wanted to be a physicist,
and I wanted to be a Shakespeare scholar.

That November
there was an important conference.
The Royal Shakespeare Company was coming.

I sat in line overnight to get the best tickets,
and I invited my friends,
Dave #1, Dave #2, and Dave #3.

Wouldn't you know it?

The real Dave
and said, "My wife is going away for the weekend.
Do you have some time you would like to spend with me?"

Away for the weekend?

I found myself babbling,
"Gee, I'm all booked up.
Maybe you have heard about the big Shakespeare conference...."

Inside
I was screaming.

He never called again.

     * * *

I still go to the McDonald's
where he worked years ago.

The building is prettier –
a neat red brick house –
but the cheeseburgers taste just the same.

Every once in a while
I drive past his old house –
a neat little gray bungalow.
Someone else lives there now,
but it looks just the same.

I hear this and that.
He has four kids.
He moved to Colorado.
His little brother was killed in a car accident.
He moved to North Carolina.

I have lost track of him.
I just don't feel the same.

The
Grudge Poems

Grudge #1: Jolene

I made it my business to know
that my boyfriend Jack
was going to a movie
with Jolene.

What sin did I commit
to deserve this?

I waited at my dorm room door all afternoon
and I heard him drop her off
at her door across the hall.

"Thank you for the milkshake,"
she said coyly.

He never bought me a milkshake.

Grudge #2: Jolene, Part 2

We were late, Jack and I
for a wedding – my friends
Michael and Kathy.

Jack insisted
upon taking a shortcut,
and we got lost.

We knew we were getting close
when we saw Jolene
cross the street.

Jack looked at Jolene,
then looked at me,
and said,
"Did you want to say something?"

I was silent
but inside
I was burning.

Grudge #3: My Birthday

Jack always gave me
unusual gifts:
an oversized pillow
a tape recorder
a little TV.

But this year was different.
He handed me
a small jewelry box.

I gasped.
"Could this be IT?"
Would he really
give me a diamond ring
in front of my whole family?

My fingers trembled
as I opened the tiny box.

It was a pair of shark's tooth earrings.
His mother picked them out.

They were the ugliest earrings I had ever seen.

Grudge #4:
The Postcard from Paris

Jack and his best friend Bob
went to Europe together
the summer after graduating from college.

I never expected
to hear from Jack again – he left
without saying good-bye.

But he sent me a postcard
from Paris:
the city of lights
the city of love.

He wrote: "We have a lot to talk about, especially me."

Later that summer
I heard Jack was back from Europe.
I called and invited him to see my play.
I was starring as Elmire in *Tartuffe*.

He had been home for two weeks,
But he hadn't called.
He didn't come to see my play.

I guess that was
The kiss-off,
The postcard from Paris.

Grudge #5: My Grandmother

I asked Jack
to come to my grandmother's funeral.

He refused,
even when I begged him to come,
for me.

No, he didn't come,
but he sent flowers – gladioli.

The flowers were lovely,
but if he had cared about me,
he would have been there for me.

I wasn't looking for it, but I had my answer.

Grudge #6: The Affair

We were in the living room,
Jack and I,
enjoying the fire in the fireplace,
when he turned to me and said,
"I had an affair
with someone else
last weekend."

I tried to hide my face
in my hands
but he held both hands
and looked into my eyes.
I felt a shadow of pain
flicker over my face.

"It's your fault," he went on,
"Because you wouldn't let me
come and see you last weekend."

I pulled my hands out from his grasp,
got up and pushed him out the front door.

I wish I could say
That I never saw him again.

Grudge #7: The Last Straw

"There's something wrong with you,"
Jack declared
just before
getting up and going out the door.

I had frozen.
I was pretending to be asleep
because I didn't know
what else to do.

Jack had touched me
just like my grandfather used to do.
I was startled,
awake
and afraid.

Maybe if I just pretended
nothing was happening....

I let him go out the door.
I closed my eyes
and said, "Good-bye, Jack."

I Must Have Loved Him

Up in the attic
I found a mysterious box
with my name on it.

I had no idea
what was inside.
But when I opened it
my heart did a swan dive
off a tall building.

It was my long-lost
stationery collection.

Tucked in among the flowered cards
I found them:
letters in Jack's handwriting.
Letters from thirty years ago.

I couldn't open the envelopes.

Summer

Summer is a-comin' in.
The sky is blue
the grass is green
and the flowers are coming up out of the ground.

Everything has changed.
I told you so, my love.
I told you it would be too late,
and nothing would be the same.

I am so sorry, my love,
but I am not waiting for you
any longer.
It is summer,
and I have a new love.

The sky is blue
the grass is green
and the flowers are coming up out of the ground.

Ice cream is on sale
half-price
at the grocery store.
In the park
parents push their babies
on the toddler swings.

The Canada geese
herd their little ones
into the water.

It is a perfect evening
for a walk around the pond.

We circle the pond
twice.
My mother
holds my hand.
The sun reflects
orange and magenta
on the water and it is summer.

Tangerine Dream

I am standing at the sink
in my perfect kitchen.
Everything matches.
The counter is tangerine
the walls are tangerine
the cabinets are tangerine
and the curtains are tangerine and white.

I am busy
scooping watermelon seeds
out of the kitchen drain
with my hands.

You approach,
and you look angry.

You might yell at me
or maybe even spank me.

I turn towards you
and you kiss me –
an electrifying kiss
that lasts an eternity.

and real life
was even better than the dream.

Apostrophe to Iced Tea

The summer drink
iced tea
you quench my thirst
in the hot, sultry summer
like no other drink.

Some prefer
peach tea, perhaps
or raspberry tea,

mango iced tea
peppermint iced tea

But the only tea for me
Is you – plain tea
unsweetened
with ice
and a slice of fresh lemon,

the cold, wet glass
pressed to my pressure points.

Summer Fruits

Peaches, strawberries,
nectarines, apricots,
dark red cherries,
green grapes,
blueberries,
raspberries,
pineapple,
watermelon,
cantaloupe,
honeydew,

Ripen
like my love for you.

Last Tango in Paris

It was my favorite movie
thirty years ago.

I was the young French girl
easily leaping over a puddle.

I was the young French girl
sucked into a sick relationship.

I was the girl
who would do absolutely anything
for love

except maybe
pull the trigger.

Heroic Love

I sent you
a book you had written,
Heroic Love.

I asked you to sign the book
and return it to me.
I even enclosed an SASE.

If Prof. S. can play Posthumus,
And you can play Iachimo,
Why can't I be Felicia?

I waited for the mail every day.
Maybe it will be today....
Or today....
Or today....

I heard the mailman
put something in the mailbox.
My heart jumped up.
I was afraid to look
but finally
I put my hand in the mailbox
and pulled out
my Visa bill.

Forgotten

I meant to bring
Felicia's book, *Victorian Marriages,* with me
on my trip to Stratford, Ontario
but I didn't have time
to check it out from the library.

"Oh well," I thought. "Oh well."

I should have read it
twenty years ago,
but I was afraid.
afraid of what I might find.

My friend Ellen
said it was a portrait
of several unhappy marriages.

Imagine my surprise
when Yuki, my traveling companion,
took it out of her bag
and began to read it.

"It's really funny," she announced.

Kirinyaga

Yesterday,
I finished writing
a book of love poems about you.

Today,
I feel lost
at loose ends
as if I have let go
of the golden thread
that holds my life
together.

Fooling around on the computer,
I decide to Google my name.
One point seven million entries,
not all of them me.

One entry
near the beginning
interests me.

My name
as a character
In a science fiction book.

Am I a hero
or a villain?
I can't tell
from the quote.

I decide
to buy the book
and read it:
Kirinyaga.

Just my luck.
It is out-of-print. I have to
special-order it.

When the book finally arrives,
I put everything else aside
and settle down
to read it carefully.

"Silent,
Upon a peak in Darien."

The Other Dark Lady

She didn't have to say it,
I already knew
although I pretended not to.
Her mother
traced their family roots
back to the court of Elizabeth I.

Emilia Lanier,
the other Dark Lady,
poet and musician,
was her ancestor.

An earthquake
opened the Grand Canyon
in my heart.

She played the part
too well.

On Shoveling Snow

I used to dream,
while shoveling snow,
of you in sunny, warm,
Southern California.
Maybe lounging by the pool
with a gin and tonic.
Maybe playing a game or two
of tennis.

I used to enjoy
dreaming of you,
even if it sometimes
made me seethe with anger
while shoveling snow.

Shoveling snow
used to epitomize
all that was wrong with my life.

After thirty years,
shoveling snow
has grown easier for me,
and harder for my parents.

Now, while shoveling snow,
I keep an eye on both of them,
knowing that
if it weren't for them,

I would be nameless,
homeless, irretrievably
lost.

Somewhere out there
in the Chicago snowstorm
there are people just like me
shivering in the cold.

I am grateful
for the light
that shines on the porch,
grateful to have a porch to shovel.

Flying

I want to fly to California
to pick silver strawberries
pink peaches
and heavy purple plums.

I want to visit
my troublesome sister.
(Why can't we ever get along?)

I want to feel the beach tar
on my feet.
I want to look out
and see
the turquoise Pacific Ocean.

Respite

Six months to a year.
The verdict was cruel, final.
No hope of reprieve
except maybe
for a dangerous procedure
that might
prolong life for a little while.

We held our breaths.

September 13, 2007,
4:30 P.M.

"His hands and feet are cold,"
whispered the minister urgently.
"He's showing all the signs."

We gathered around the hospital bed
in my parents' bedroom.

I took his hand in mine.
We watched every heartbeat,
every breath.

His eyes rolled up twice.
There was a single catch in his throat.

The minister said, "Let's pray."

"Our Father...."

Miraculous

I stopped at my favorite McDonald's,
had a cheeseburger and a Coke.

When I went up to the fountain
to refill my cup
my rings flew off my finger
in two different directions.

I watched as the gold wedding band
bounced and rolled ten or twelve feet
and came to rest
near the manager's shoe.
Youthful, attractive, auburn-haired,
she resembled a stewardess
in her brown polyester uniform
with a neat cream tie at her neck.

"Pretty," she said.
I picked up the ring
and put it back on.

But where was the other ring?
I looked under all the tables
in the immediate area.
Nothing.

I looked under the fountain.
Nothing but a clean, bare floor.

A white-haired couple
sitting in a nearby booth
joined the search.

Another manager,
a young, African-American man,
comforted me;
We will find it," he said, determined.

I was just about ready to give up
When a middle-aged lady asked me,
"What are you looking for?"

"A diamond ring," I answered,
and she held it up.

The First Spring Without My Father

Death took him ever so gently.
We were all there.
I held his hand.

The hospice nurse
said to tell him
it was okay to let go.

He didn't want to go.
I didn't want him to go.

But he turned his attention
to the business of dying
and in a few minutes
those deep blue eyes
that I loved so well
lost their light
and settled into a fixed stare.

It was early fall,
the sun still warm,
the leaves and trees still green.

* * *

The soldiers played "Taps,"
and folded the American floag.

The casket
touched the bottom of the grave.

"Oh, no," I thought.
"Please don't put the earth back
on top of the casket.
I don't think I can bear it."

They didn't. Not then.

But when we came back
the next day
a blanket of new earth
covered the grave.

"Oh, no," I thought.
"Not my dad."

When I walked over the grave
to put flowers in the vase
my foot
sank deep into the soft ground
surrounding him.

* * *

Over the long winter months
his spirit was still with us
somehow.

As I poured my tea,
I could hear him say,
"Don't forget
to agitate the teabag
a little in the cup."

But now
in the first few days
of the first spring without him
my dad is gone.

Everything else is coming back to life.
I don't know why,
but somehow I expected
he would come back, too.

Warm spring breeze,
caress the soft, damp earth.
Cover him lightly,
gentle earth.

Random Thoughts

He died by degrees, inch by inch.
Diabetes.
Heart trouble.
Stomach cancer.
Liver cancer.

We sorrowed slowly with him
every step of the way.

We said good-bye in steps:
the closing of the casket,
the pallbearers
putting the flag-covered burden
into the waiting hearse.

We all stayed
until the casket
touched the ground
lowered all the way.

      * * *

When we came back the first time
the earth was filled in
and the flowers
carelessly
thrown on top.

When we came back
the second time

there was a blanket of fresh sod
over the grave.

We put fall flowers
into the vase.

When we go back
next time
we will put a holly wreath
over the snow.

Christmas

no silver bells
no snow

no long lines
at the department stores

not a lot of money
for presents

dinner at my sister's
instead of at home

one empty place
at the head of the table

still
the Christmas of the heart
will endure.

Memorial Day

The weatherman
predicted rain all day.

But we set out,
my mom, my brother, and I,
to bring flowers
and an American flag
to put on my father's grave.

My father never talked much
about his military career,
but I know he served in Korea
and the occupation of Japan.

While he was in Korea,
he gave his one hot meal
every day
to an orphan in a nearby village.

We put the spring bouquet in the vase
and sat on the marble bench
for a little while.

"Well, dear," my mother said,
"Here we are.
I wish we could visit with you."

I wanted to say,
"I miss you, Dad,"

but the rain
began to fall.

I don't want to write about...

My father.
It's been over a year now
and I still cry when I think about him.

I said I had no regrets.
My mom and I did everything we could for him.
Still, sometimes
we had to leave him alone
for a long time.

My sister came every day.
He would say,
"Is Annalisa coming today?"

The day he died
the minister said every member of the family
should tell him it was okay to go,
that we would be all right.

But I didn't.
I couldn't.
I knew I would cry
and then he would cry
and neither one of us wanted to cry.

So I held his hand,
and said nothing.

What She Needs

It is a gray day.
I am wearing gray.

The three of us
are visiting Maggie
in the nursing home.

The only touches of color
are Chelsea's gold fleece tunic
and Marta's multicolored sweater.
Red, green, purple.

Maggie is sleeping.
I don't want to wake her
but we do.

We read poems aloud
and suddenly the room is filled
with seductive teenagers,
a girl and her little brother "The Tornado."
Nonno and his keychain,
a poem about a poem.

Maggie nods off.

Chelsea, Marta, and I
look at each other.
"This is what she needs," we agree.

Every Day

On my way to work
I pass the cemetery
and I think of him.
It's been a long time –
three years –
but my eyes still get blurry
when I pass the gates.

I keep on going
have to go to work
and the tears dry
on my cheeks.

Every day
on my way home from work
I pass the hospital
and I think of her.

Was this hospital
the last thing she saw?

Did they bring her here
in an ambulance?

Were the lights flashing,
the sirens screaming,
or was all silent?

Yellow Tulips

I think abut my dad
more often than I let on.

I think my mom does, too.
But we go about our business
every day
without mentioning him
or how much we miss him.

This is the third spring
since he passed away.

I don't know what to say,
so I buy her
yellow tulips.

To My Father

Before he left us
I thought, like Natalie Cole
sang of her father,
"He was too good to be true."
I thought,
"No one will ever take his place."
I thought,
"I will never get over this."

But the days followed one another
like footsteps on a long journey
and the tears eventually stopped falling.

His toothbrush and razor
still stand in the medicine cabinet.

His old slippers
still hide in the closet.

His voice
still answers the phone
after three rings.

He is the Bible
I will never close
and put on the shelf.

Taking the Train into the City

Brings back memories.
The time I missed the train
and my dad
raced
to the next stop
and the next stop
and the one after that
until I finally made it,
meeting Jack.

Somehow
my dad
always knew
what train I'd be on
on my way home
and there he was
in his Chevrolet
waiting for me.

War Dream

I was hiding in a corner
in a room full of people.
It was a waiting room,
but there was no doctor.

Out the window
I could see the enemy forces
taking command.

My father and mother
were waiting together.
I waited alone in the corner.

A woman in a nurse's uniform
took people out of the room
one by one.

My father and mother
left together.

I was alone
with a stranger.

The nurse took the stranger
and then came to me.

My father went out a hero,
and my mother, too.

"If it's up to me," I said,
"I will give my life for my country

but I would rather be
shot in the heart
than beheaded."

"You don't have that choice," she replied.

Missing My Dad

I am just
sitting on the steps
in the basement stairwell –
my favorite spot.

I am just
smoking and woolgathering.

I notice
dirty leaves and dried grass
at the bottom of the stairwell.

If my father were here,
he would probably tell me
to sweep up the leaves and grass.

"You're not doing anything anyway,"
he would say.

I would be a little annoyed,
But I would eventually do it.

But my dad isn't here.

I smoke a little longer,
look at the leaves and grass,
and go to get the broom.

I'm not really doing anything anyway.

The Language of Flowers

I was not there with him
In the doctor's office
but I know how my dad always
set his jaw
when he was rally angry.

The doctor had made a mistake
and my dad, who had already
been through so much –
a triple bypass
and chemotherapy –
was going to die.

"Doctors bury their mistakes,"
he said to me when he got home.
He had said the same thing to the doctor.

"I don't want any flowers
when they plant me," he said bitterly.
"No flowers."

His words came back to me
when we put the huge cascade
of red roses
over the casket.

The gold letters
on the red satin ribbon
read, "Dearest Father."

My Father's Sunglasses

They were the clip-on kind.

He clipped them onto his regular glasses
early in the morning
when he drove east to work
and he clipped them on again
when he drove west to come home.

My teenage self thought,
"Why does he wear
those dumb clip-on sunglasses?"

Now, in my expensive prescription sunglasses,
I drive east to work,
and west to come home.

While I am driving –
with the glare of the sun in my eyes
both ways –
I think about
the braces my dad bought me
to straighten my teeth,
the violin and the violin lessons
my dad paid for,
the college education,
both undergraduate
and graduate school,
and the medcal bills,
the many, many medical bills.

And I love those damned, stupid
clip-on sunglasses.

Part I: "Friends"

My dad
drove a silver Chevrolet Caprice.

He used to call the other cars
on the road
his "friends."

I drive a baby-blue Toyota Corolla.
I must drive like an old lady
because the other cars
tailgate me,
pass me,
and cut in front of me.

Not exactly my "friends."

Sometimes I see them
down the road a little
stopped by police
with the red Mars lights flashing.

Part II: Traffic

Years ago,
every time I heard a car horn,
I figured they were honking at me,
so I would jump, step on the gas,
and shoot out into traffic
without looking.

Now,
whenever I hear a car horn,
I mutter to myself,
just like my dad,
"So what else did you get for Christmas?"

The Little Black Dress

I bought it on a whim,
a simple dress
with rosettes on the shoulder.

I wore it to a Christmas party.
It looked great
with black tights
and black patent leather shoes.

I washed it
according to the instructions:
hand wash, cold water, line dry.

It was a little wrinkled,
so I put it in the dryer
with a wet towel
for ten minutes.

"Oops!" One of the rosettes came off
and the glue
smeared all ovef the sleeve.

I tried to get it off with nail polish remover.
No luck.

What would Daddy have done?
I looked over his workbench:
Gumout, turpentine, paint thinner,
Windex, silver polish, pine cleaner,
plant food, bug spray, Scotchgard.

Then I looked in his cabinet
above the laundry tubs.
"Oops!" for clothes.
gets out crayon, lipstick, adhesive.
The perfect thing!

I followed the directions:
put the dress on a towel, dabbed it with "Oops!"
and the glue magically disappeared!

Fun 101

In the afternoon
on a Monday

the little red MG
pulled into
the McDonald's lot

parked in the
handicapped spot.

An older couple
got out.

She wore a blue-green
chiffon scarf

and he had on
a gray golfer's cap.

She ordered
a hot fudge sundae.

He had
a free senior coffee.

They were laughing together
as they left,

put the top down on the car
and drove away.

The license plate
read "FUN 101."

Surprise!

"You're going to be a great-aunt!"
Amie cried over the phone.
"Gramma is going to be a great-grandma!"

I told her I was surrpised,
and she said, "YOU were surprised!"

We laughed together.

"Do you know whether it's a boy or a girl?"

"We want to be surprised."

And I thought about
that precious little heart
beating.

You are Already Loved

It was hard to love a sonogram at first.
In the early stages
you looked like snow on TV.

Then your body
started to take shape,
your shoulders, your head.
Fingers and toes.

But when I saw your cute little face
for the first time
on the sonogram,
you looked just like your mom
when she was a baby

and

I felt a tiny flower
blossom in my heart.

Pink Cupcakes

Annalisa invited us to a party
for Amie and her new baby, Scarlett.
Our first meeting with the baby.
Our first chance in six months to see Amie.

Everyone brought presents.
Great-Gramma Joan
brought a pink "Hello, Kitty" cat,
pink baby doll,
pink teddy bear.

Great-Great Auntie Doris
brought a tiny soft pink skirt and top,
the perfect size: 3 to 6 months.

Great-Auntie Mary
brought a bright pink tutu
with pink ballet socks
and a pink flowered headband.
Her daughters, both ballerinas,
picked them out.

"Who wants to hold the baby?"
asked Amie.

"I do!"
"I do!"
"I do!"

Great-Gramma Joan took the first turn,
Great-Great Auntie Doris was next,
then came Great-Auntie Barbara – me!

I held little Scarlett
over my shoulder
with a rose-pink blanket
and patted her back very gently.

She weighed about seven pounds.
She was so warm.
She fell asleep.

Amie put a pillow under my arm
so I wouldn't get tired.

I held Scarlett until the pizza came.
Cheese, pepperoni, and veggie.
Hot, fresh, and delicious.

But the plum, the smasher, the coup
the pièce de résistance,
was the dessert:
pink cupcakes
placed like works of art
on tiered dishes.

Yellow cakes
covered in light pink frosting
with hot pink sprinkles
around the edges.

Does Amie like pink?
"Bring it on!" Amie exclaimed, smiling.

Long-Distance Romance And Further Dreams

True Love in Westmont

I used to dream
that one day I'd grow up
and have a nice man
to take me
to a little place near my house
where they have neon lights
and jazz and frog legs every Friday night.

That little place
is a dry cleaners now.

Long-Distance
Romance
Swing Dancing

I Saw You Around, Part I

I saw you around
near the science buildings,
Morrill and Burrill Hall,
and in the mailroom.

Those moments
were moments
of heightened awareness.

I felt I was
in the presence of
someone who was highly intelligent –
and icy.

The cold
sent shivers
up my spine.

Where was it
that it happened,
that first glance?

I didn't know your name,
but I could tell
that you were someone important.

Where were we?
On the Quad,
outside the English Building?
It doesn't matter.

But I will never forget
how your eyes sought mine,
and locked me into
an invisible embrace.

I felt my eyes
grow wide,
looking up into your own.

Our eyes twisted
onto a single string,
a double stare.

I couldn't speak.

The only thought
I could muster
was, "WOW!!!
I could so easily
fall in love with you –
I am half in love
with you already."

I Saw You Around, Part II

And I thought,
"WOW!!! That guy could
make me give up
my life's dream."

So I avoided you.

Something inside me
said, "Watch out!
That guy is
BIG TROUBLE!"

But I saw you around,
and I said "Hi,"
once or twice.

I heard you were
a Shakespeare scholar.
That's what I wanted to be.

You looked like a Shakespeare scholar,
a handsome, young
aspiring Hamlet.

I remember seeing your name
in the schedule of classes,
but I didn't put
two and two together.

"What a nice name,"
I thought.

"He's new. He's really good,"
a fellow student exulted.
So I signed up.

It was the first day
of class,
and I was late.

I stood in the doorway
and saw you
at the head of the class.

A pretty, blonde
young woman
came down the center aisle
into your arms
and kissed you
right on the mouth.

You blushed, and
I thought,
"What a wonderful man
he must be."
And I put
two and two together.

"What a wonderful man
he must be," I thought
again,
and I wished I were
that pretty, blonde
girl.

I'll never forget
that moment,
everything falling into place,
the name and the face,
standing at the threshold
and falling in love with you
head over heels.

The Changeling

You asked for volunteers.

I was always the first to raise my hand.

I would be Beatrice-Joanna,

and a young man I didn't know,

a fellow students,

was to play Deflores.

The student reminded me of a toad,

even though he was handsome,

in a way,

and he glowed with youth.

This young man and I presented a stage picture:

me on my knees,

my back to the class,

and Deflores standing over me,

facing the audience.

I implored him to help me

in my quest

to marry Alsemero,

another character.

"I will do anything," I pleaded.

Suddenly, I was aware

of someone's eyes on my back

of someone's eyes on my bottom.

I could feel

your confident

malevolent glance.

"This teacher doesn't seem to be very smart,"
I thought. "But he sure is cute.
I bet I could wrap him around my little finger.
Too bad I have a steady boyfriend,
and he is dating Elena Lennox."

I don't know how it happened,
but suddenly you became Deflores,
and I turned into Beatrice-Joanna,
and I pledged to you
that I would do absolutely anything for you.

And that was how it all began.

Going to Santa Barbara

I have never been on an airplane.
Tomorrow I will fly 2,000 miles
to Santa Barbara, California
to see you, although I pretend
that is not the reason.

Tonight I will pack,
night will turn into day,
and I will be in Santa Barbara
tomorrow.

I can't believe it's true.

The takeoff is exciting.
We pass over the Grand Canyon,
and the sky turns red.

Here I am in Santa Barbara!!!
They have McDonald's in California, too!!!

I am driving a blue Toyota Celica
through the mountains.
When I reach the coast,
the air is fresh with the ocean breeze.
It is so real. It is too much.

The streets are lined with palm trees.
I have never seen so many palm trees.
The sky is turquoise.
Boys are hang-gliding over the ocean.

You said to look for a shopping center.
Is this the one?
No, not yet. Yes, this is it.
I make a left turn,
and there is your house:
a California ranch
with a bright yellow MG in front,
just as you said.

Should I stay in my car?
Should I knock at the door?
It is so real.
It is too much.

You answer the door.
You give me a kiss.
You hand me a piña colada
and say, "I would like to make love to you,
but I can't take on a dependent right now."

I throw the piña colada
in your face.
You cut out my heart
with a pair of scissors.

It is so real.
It is too much.

I drive back to Los Angeles
and fly back home to Chicago.

Have I really been to Santa Barbara?
Am I really back home in Chicago?

I am changed forever.

September: A Substitute Teacher's Love Song

The Shakespeare poster
on the classroom wall
is a message from you.

(I imagine you traveling 2,000 miles
and getting up early to tack it here.)

An article on marriage customs in India
from the social studies class
is a sign that you are near:
I can almost touch your touch.

The Monet postcard
next to the school receptionist's desk
echoes the water lilies card I sent you.

The picture of Hemingway, bearded,
smoking a pipe,
is your portrait.

Images re-group.
The colored pictures multiply and advance.

I imagine an angry man behind each one
of a million Shakespeare posters.
I promise to leave you alone
if you will leave me alone.

The poster falls, an empty card –
I see only Ernest Hemingway, leaving.

October: Halloween

It's Halloween, and the street are filled with
small, strange shapes.
Their strangeness hurts.

I call you long-distance from a phone booth,
just to hear your voice,
just to hear you say, "Hello."
I hang up. I can't talk.
You live in a new fantasy.

There is a conference this weekend
at the University of Chicago.
Wayne Booth will speak on feminism.
I see witches in the sky, and I am
one of them.

A man and a woman come to speak to me at school.
The man is silent but he shakes my hand.
Only the woman speaks.
An old friend, Mike, calls during this interview,
and I am a little short with him on the phone.
The woman nods her approval.
I am a witch.

If only you would love me.
I am divine.
The Renaissance is coming; men and women
will soon love each other again.
The mind/body problem is solved.

Love is a concrete word.

God is neither male nor female.

The old tales are simply old tales,
but they have a spark of truth.

The new religion is coming.

November: Thanksgiving

I didn't think about you
When I bought the Heinekens,
ordered the cake, the travel posters, and
the T-shirt that said,
"Well-loved American novelist."

I didn't think about you.
It was a going-away party
for my best friend.
We drank beer, danced to "Sweet Dreams,"
and sang along with the B-52's,
"They lay down the law in Mesopotamia."
We had a good time.
I didn't think about you.

But when I heard
that you were giving a party,
I couldn't help wondering
if you still drank Dewar's
and smoked a pipe;
if you made the hors d'oeuvres yourself;
if you still hesitated when you talked;
if you and your friends had a good time.

I didn't think about you.
I had a good time.

But I couldn't help wondering
If perhaps the chair next to yours
was empty, too.

December: Charlie Chaplin's The Gold Rush

I flew to Alaska to meet you,
in a new red coat with black trim,
like the charmingly clumsy
Muscovites in *Love's Labor's Lost,*
dancing to win hearts
dancing for love.

I shoveled a lot of snow
to pay for that New Year's Eve party.
I placed a folded napkin next to
each plate, but
no one came.
I waited up all night, and dreamt
I was dancing the "Oceana Roll,"
party favors and all.

All I remember now
is that, in parting, I sent you
white roses.

My poor white roses,
dashed
like a Christmas comedy.

January: Torch Song

I will forget you this year,
forget about the nectarines
you gave me,
first fruits from your young tree,
about the violets
you watered so tenderly
in the arbor in your back yard.

I will forget about the sandcastle we made
on the shores of the Pacific Ocean,
about the beach tar
you washed off my feet.

I saved the nectarines,
set them in the sun
and ate them when they ripened,
one by one.
I wonder what became of the violets.
No doubt the sandcastle
vanished silently
when the tide came in
that same evening
several years ago.

It's the first night of the New Year
and tonight
I am dining alone
in the magnificent lobby
of a fine hotel.

I eat fresh bay scallops
and drink Scotch,
trying to recapture for one last moment
the memory of the first evening
we spent together

Even though the pianist plays
all the love songs I know
and even though
this is my second
or third Scotch,
your chair is still empty.

February: Valentine

"I love you," I said to the bodiless voice
over the wire.
"Is that you, Barbara? The operator told me
it was an emergency.
I was talking to my father."

"I'm sorry."

The wire was silent for a moment
but then I heard
a sigh.
"Look, I like you very much,
but I *certainly* don't love you."

"All right."
It was not all right.

"Are you all right?"
"Yes." Then, "No, I feel terrible."

Words, something soothing, I don't
remember what
reached me eventually, and I
hung up. Not before asking,
I am ashamed to say,
if we could be friends
for a long time.

And you have answered every one
of my letters
for several years now.

Why do you write back?

March: The Visit

Is there any truth to the rumor
that you blew in with the snow?
The snow's still here.

There was a party, I remember.
I wasn't really invited, but
I knew you would be there.

The guest of honor was put out
because he was a little upstaged.
One woman made a pointed remark
about party-crashers,
I think I embarrassed my best friend.

All for a kiss on the cheek.

April: "No Romance"

I have had the same dream all my life:
I am married to Bluebeard,
wife number eight.

He locks me up every morning
before he goes to work
to do whatever Bluebeards do.

One day, he leaves the key
within my reach,
but I realize
it is because he loves me
so I stay.

Once I was in the library after you
and the librarian showed me
the card for the book you checked out,
Hero and Saint.
"He doesn't know it," I confided,
"But he's my hero."
We heard a door slam
and I knew it was you.

Now I dream about you.
Your hair is long and tied back
behind your neck.

The full professors are taking you
out to the quadrangle
to chop off your head.

I run down the library stairs
out into the sunshine.

There is still time
for me to save you.

May: Long-Distance

If I grow my hair long,
If I read the books that you have read,
If I remember to check the weather
in your part of the country
every night,
If I make all the green lights
on my way home,
If I remember to look at the sunset
every night,
If I should happen to look up at the stars
and if,
at the same moment,
you are looking at the same star,
then maybe I will see you again.

No Walk in the Park

Spring is not the time
for this kind of love.

The unrequited kind
is out of fashion now.

An elderly couple
sits on the park bench
shading their eyes
as they watch their grandchildren
play in the sun.

He wears a gray wool cap
and smokes a pipe.
A cane
rests on the bench
next to her knee.

You must be bored
with being worshipped
from afar.

If I really loved you
I suppose
I would let you go.

Only I keep thinking
of new ways
to say good-bye:
just one more phone call

just one more letter
just one more poem.

If only you....
but, break, my heart,
For I must hold my tongue.

My Poetic Process

I cleaned all day.
No time to think about
blue eyes
and a gold sweater.

But the funniest thing
I found myself
thinking about
your blue eyes
and your gold sweater
and I cleaned all day.

My fingers flew....
sorting out papers
discarding old journals
and finding poems about you
in the oddest places:
jewelry box
dresser drawers
under the bed.

Your sweater was gold,
your hair was light brown,
and your eyes were blue.

I sweep the floor,
mop under the bed,
and organize drawers
and jewelry box.

I find myself
thinking about
a party
twenty-three years ago.
You drank Dewar's.
I drank Johnnie Walker Red.

Who could have predicted
all that would happen
after that first kiss?

I pile the library books
into the bookshelf.
All about Shakespeare.
Half of a poem
sticks out of *Hamlet*.
There are poems about you
in the Monet stationery box....

Would I have
hitched my star
to your starship
twenty-three years ago
if I had known
what would happen?

My life has been
one long love poem.

"Yes," I said, "yes,"
to the blue eyes
and the gold sweater.

I followed you out to the landing,
and kissed you again,
not knowing what would happen.

Would I do it all again?
I am finished cleaning.
The room is spotless.

I find one more poem
hidden under my pillow.
It is about your blue eyes
and your gold sweater.

Traveling in my Sleep

I am driving from Chicago to the University of Maryland,
leaving home to go back to graduate school.

For some reason, I must go through Duluth,
which, in my dream, is on the way.

I stop to take a swim.
It is winter
and the green pool water is chilly.
It must be 40 degrees below zero
but I hope to swim 100 laps
before I continue on my journey.

I decide to go south on the Beltway to Montgomery College
where I teach part-time.
The drive is long
and I am going the long way around,
but the job is worth it.
I am lucky to have the job.

When I get out of the car,
I begin walking,
looking for my old high school,
but I find myself
in the cafeteria
of my junior high.

I am teaching eighth grade
and I discover
that I haven't finished junior high.

I am an adult
In a cafeteria full of children.

Half-sleeping, half-awake,
I find myself
playing Titania
in *A Midsummer Night's Dream,*
but the scenery isn't painted
and I haven't learned my lines.

New Scars

I thought
It couldn't happen again.
Nothing ever like it –
a revolver
exploding
at the back of my head.

What could happen to me after you?

I tried to stay the same for many years.
Then I cut my hair, my middle thickened,
I stopped wearing contact lenses
started wearing holiday sweaters.

What could happen to me after you?

I cut my knee while I was shaving my legs.
My hair turned gray.
My forehead wrinkled.

My father had a triple bypass.

What could happen to me after you?

Bedtime Story

Maybe it's time for me to leave you.
Maybe it's time for me to give up.
Maybe that's the healthy thing to do.

I have visions of a new life:
No guilt, no worries, no you.

I will exercise every day. Lose those extra pounds.
I will throw myself into my work;
Write a new poem every day.

Yes,
I see my new life taking shape already.

But in my mind's eye
you reach out to me
I take your hand
and fall back into bed.

At Long Last, Love

How shall I say good-bye this time, this last?
No more letters, no more phone calls now.
We weren't really lovers, and it's past,
You seem to have forgotten me, somehow.

Saying good-bye might cause you to recall
What you have long ago forgotten, love –
That you loved me, and you loved me not at all.
That I loved you; that it was and wasn't love.

Even still, I feel a need to let you know,
To tell you honestly, at last, my love –
That, at long last, love, I am letting you go,
Setting you free from guilt, from pain, from love.

I promised not to call or write, it seems,
So I will tell you tonight, in my dreams.

Further Dreams

Blue Nightmare, Part I

All my life, I've had the same nightmare –
exactly the same,
every time,
over and over again.

I am riding on the train alone.
I am a very small girl, maybe four or five.
I have blue eyes and blonde hair.
The air is blue with smoke.
I am alone.

I am sitting on the aisle.
The train is full of big, older men.
They are smoking cigars.

I am wearing a little blue plaid dress.
I have a warm coffeecake on my lap,
and there is a note pinned to my shoulder.
I do not know what the note says.
I do not recognize anyone on the train.
I am alone on a train full of strangers.
Where am I going?

Am I sleeping?
Where are Mama and Daddy?
Am I going to Aunt Anna Mae's house?
Where does she live?
Will I ever see Mama and Daddy again?

The dream has fuzzy edges.
The darkness of my memory swallows the dream,
but the nightmare
always comes back –
exactly the same, every time,
over and over again.

Blue Nightmare, Part II

"POETRY MAKES NOTHING HAPPEN."
W. H. AUDEN

It's a nightmare.
My blue nightmare.
Again.

I am four years old.
I am alone on a train.

It's a nightmare.

Blue smoke....old men....cigars....
My new blue plaid dress....
Warm coffeecake on my lap....
Note pinned to my shoulder....
Mama and Daddy, where are you?

It's a nightmare.

Forty years later,
I turn on the light and reach for a pen.
My nightmare pours out on the page.

I have to get it out, get it all out
in a poem.

In the morning
I show the poem to my mother.
She says, "Yes, it really happened."
We talk, and a miracle takes place:
I never have that nightmare again.

Renaissance Hero

I had a dream about you before I knew you.

Professor Gargoyle
shut the gray wooden door of his office.

Only he and I
were inside
with the tapestry rug
and the carved wooden table.

He lifted me up,
put me on the table,
and just in time
to save me
from being ravished
you appeared
the Renaissance hero
to the Medieval villain.

But it was only a dream.

In real life,
I stepped lightly back from Professor Gargoyle's kiss
told him I had a student waiting
and went directly down to your office.

You weren't there.

Dream Weaver

I spin fantasies
Jasmine dreams
Water lily fictions

All about you, my love.
All about you.

My daydreams
climb snowy Himalayan mountains.

My nightdreams
rest in warm California pools.

All about you, my love.
All about you.

I spin fantasies
Water lily fictions
Jasmine dreams

Because the truth
is too cruel
to be real.

R.S.V.P.

You are welcome
by special invitation only
to dip your toes
into the warm bath.

Come on in,
the water's fine.

Up to your ankles?
The water is hot, hot, hot
but not too hot.

Come on in,
stretch out your length.

Relax,
there's room for us both
in the lavender and mint.

For Cecy

In the dark, moonlit forest
I finally see you
walking on glowing white
Hansel-and-Gretel pebbles
in the blue-black velvet night.

I want to ask where you are going,
child of the moon and stars,
but I remember.

I understand the wind is calling you,
and the winged falcon-horse is waiting
to carry you through the sky,
the silver forest,
and violin music's time.

But before you go,
let me give you opals,
beautiful as tears.
Before you go,
please walk with me
among the stars
once more.

Cinderella Story

I dreamt
I was going to a formal dance
at Century 21 – the fanciest hotel
in Champaign, Illinois.

I got all dressed up
in my long
midnight blue dress
and I found
a lot of counterfeit money
I planned to spend.

It was late,
10 P.M.,
but I still wasn't ready.

Someone told me,
"No one will be there
until midnight."

Someone told me,
"Your true love
will be there tonight."

It was late,
midnight,
and I couldn't find my earrings,
I couldn't find my lipstick.
Someone had stolen my purse.

The White Girl

(A PAINTING BY JAMES MCNEILL WHISTLER)

She stands alone.
She is all in white.
White on white.
A long, Victorian dress
with puffed sleeves
and lace at the neck.

She is all in white.
White on white.
The ribbon about her waist
is white.
The curtains behind her
are white.
She holds a single white lily, wilting.

She is all in white.
White on white.
Her long dark hair
is slightly mussed
as if she has just removed a veil.

She is all alone.

Strange Dream: Love Triangle

I always thought it was marvelous –
your house had a red Dutch door
that opened onto a courtyard.

In my dream,
a giraffe
stood in your courtyard.

You – the man of the house –
climbed up onto the roof.

You held out your hand to the giraffe
who joined you on the roof
and then you both
jumped to the ground.

You and the giraffe
walked across the yard
to me
and we stood there,
all three together,
silhouetted by the sun.

She – the lady of the house –
walked across the yard
to us
and we ran inside
looking out the window
of a large house
that wasn't ours.

She crossed her arms and said,
"You should really clean up that mess."

We picked up our potato chip bags
and Coke bottles
and silently stole away.

Further Dreams

You come to me in dreams
every night
even though
you are two thousand miles away.
Father than dreams can reach.
So far away.

Your last letter
was dated July 3rd
seven years ago.

I know you hate to write letters,
but still....
So far away from you – so far away.

I mailed your birthday card
this morning
to the last address I have for you.
Will it come back
"Return to Sender"?
So far away – away from you – so very far away.

I checked your name on the internet.
forty-four references,
some of them not yours.
But your books are still in print.
What are you working on now?
I have no way of knowing.

I feel so far away from you.

So, far be distant, sweet friend.

I will not call, I will not write.
Still I send my dreams further and further
every night.

Dreams of Milk

I found myself shopping
In an organiz grocery store
With Patrice and Dan,
A couple I knew from college.

I needed a gallon of milk.
Everywhere I looked
there were huge glass bottles of milk
heavy as cream.
The price of a gallon:
$97.00.

"Ninety-seven dollars for a gallon of milk!"
I protested.

Patrice said she would help me
find some cheaper milk
so I left my cart in the aisle
and went with her and Dan.

When I returned with the milk,
my cart had disappeared
along with my wallet, all my money,
IDs, and credit cards.

In the spot
where the cart had been
was my old violin case.

I opened the case
and inside
I found my wallet
with everything in it.

Scrambled

Naked,
except for a white cotton apron,
I am serving scrambled eggs
to three men
seated at the counter
in a family-style restaurant.

Scrambled eggs
for Jack, my ex-boyfriend,
who cheated on me
and said it was my fault.

More scrambled eggs
for Professor Martin, a Shakespeare friend,
who got angry
when I failed to tell him
that my mentor (his friend)
had passed away.

Even more scrambled eggs –
"all-you-can-eat" scrambled eggs –
For Hamlet
Who made love to me
and then told me he didn't love me.

Close Your Eyes

The temperature is 75 degrees
the sun is gently shining
there is a delicate cool breeze
and it is like this
every day
in Santa Barbara.

I sleep late,
pad to the kitchen in bare feet
leisurely drink coffee with milk
wash my hair
dry it in the sun
and think about you
and Santa Barbara.

I write poems all day
take a break
play with the dog
grill steaks outside for dinner.
I could do this
every day
in Santa Barbara.

The orange and magenta sunset
is somehow sexy.
Sexy, too,
are the long, brown arms
of the Santa Inez mountains.

I close my eyes.
It is midnight
and I am in Santa Barbara.

Ophelia's Dream

Last night
I dreamt I was visiting England
looking for Hamlet.

The houses
were piled on top of one another
and the rooms were tiny.
It seemed there was no way out.

Rosencrantz and Guildenstern
directed me to a library
where Hamlet
was conducting a small class.

My heart went out to him.

Claudius and Laertes
lectured hundreds of dutiful students
while Hamlet
sat on the edge of his desk
and kept an audience of fifteen
rapt.

Hamlet said I could stay with him
for twenty pounds a month
and I agreed.

We went to a door
that opened out onto the Atlantic Ocean.
The white-capped waves were frozen.

Child of My Father, Child of My Love

The poem won't come.
It's about cancer
and my father.
I have a lot to say
but my thoughts are like a child
who has yet to be born.

I coax the poem into being born.
The poem starts to come
like a shy child.
My father has cancer.
I don't know what else to say.
I am worried about my father.

I have always been close to my father.
He has been my hero ever since I was born.
There's not much else one can say.
The poem is starting to come....
The doctors say they got all the cancer.
I have never felt so helpless, like a child.

I should have had a child.
A boy, just like my father.
Will my father survive cancer?
Will my child every be born?
If I ask my love to come, will he come?

If I ever see my love again, will I know what to say?
If I ever see my love again, what will he say?
Does he want a child?
If I ask him to come, will he come?
No one could ever take the place of my father....
Still, there is always happiness when a child is born.
If only my father could be cured of his cancer....

The doctors say they got all the cancer.
We caught it early, the doctors say.
Will my father live to know my child?
Will I keep my promise to look after my father?
Come, my love, come.

I say, come, my love, come.
I say, you will survive this cancer, Father.
The child is a poem newborn.

The Phoenix and the Turtledove

I slip quietly
out the back basement door
and perch
in my favorite spot
on the top step.

The sky is a huge shadow.
The trees are darker shadows.
I am a shadow, too.

I look for the constellation of Orion
and the North Star.
You are Orion,
and I am the North Star.
We are far apart.

The neighbors are still sleeping.
The newspaper will come soon.

First one up
makes the coffee
warm and bittersweet.
My body is waking up.

I used to
dream away the time
but now I rise with the lark.

Wait – is that a nightingale I hear?

I have never heard the nightingale sing
yet I know
the nightingale sings in the dark.

Wait – is it the nightingale or the lark?

You are the nightingale
and I am the lark.
We may never meet again.

It is getting light.
The sparrows are waking up, too.
And the skittery pigeons.

Did Mark Antony and Cleopatra
ever meet secretly at dawn?

You are the Arabian bird,
and I am the turtledove.

You might arrive at any moment.
I hear your voice,
and my heart is suspended in mid-air —
it is early morning
and I am in love.

Three Visions from Shakespeare's Cymbeline

Vision I

"HANG THERE LIKE FRUIT, MY SOUL,
'TIL THE TREE DIE." (V, V, 263-4)

I was at the bookstore
with my father, Cymbeline, the king,
when I saw you –

Posthumus – the hero,
just after the battle
with rumpled clothes
and a three days' beard.

But your eyes
ah – your eyes
pierced the air boldly
overmastering my own
frightened stare.

I looked away,
the heroine, Imogen,
refusing to acknowledge Posthumus
until after the issues were resolved.

I found my father
at the end of the aisle
and showed him my selection,
Women's Re-visions of Shakespeare.

Was it really you?
My heart, oh my heart.
My mind, oh my mind.
My thoughts flew
quickly and gently as starlight.

Should I buy *Reviving Ophelia?*
Black Ophelia?
I Know Why the Caged Bird Sings?

When I looked again,
you were gone.

Vision II: Acting Iachimo

There was a noise in the dark.
I was sleeping.
Someone was coming up the stairs.
It sounded like my father,
but it was not my father.
It was you, Posthumus.

You carried a flashlight.
I could see your face
as you rummaged in my dresser drawers.
I felt the chill of fright.
"What do you want?" I asked.

There was no answer.
You played the villain –
Iachimo – sneaking into
Imogen's bedchamber
while she slept.

A smile touched my lips gently
and I fell back asleep.

Vision III: The Ending

I went over to my sister's house
to watch the Walt Disney *Hercules* video
with my niece, Katie.
We were all three entranced by the film.

The god Hercules
falls in love with a mortal woman,
saves her life,
and stays on Earth with her.

My sister's husband
was walking back and forth
doing some office work.

I could have sworn
that he disappeared into the bedroom
and you – Posthumus –
walked across the room.

I called you "Will,"
and asked if you had seen the video.

I wanted you to come and sit by me,
but I was afraid to ask.

Was it you,
or was it Will?

My sister and her husband,
Meg and Hercules.

Are you playing Posthumus in *Cymbeline,*
The happiest ending in the world,
Or the Prince of Denmark in *Hamlet,*
Shakespeare's greatest tragedy?

I Dream of France

France is so far away....
Why France, my love?

In my dream, you live in France.
Always in France, my love.

You write *L'amour Héroïque,*
you are married again,
this time to a Parisienne,
and you dedicate your books to her.

In my dream,
I am in Stratford-upon-Avon,
trying to cross to Paris.
I am at the train station, lost my luggage,
missed the last train.

The Royal Shakespeare Company actors advise me,
"Leave him alone. He is happily married.
He loves le Mont Sant-Michel."

In my dream,
I never get to France.
J'ai oubli'e tout mon francais.

I have forgotten all my French.

Why France, my love?
So far away....

Research

A little voice
told me
I'd better not do it.

That same little voice
told me
I'd be sorry.

But I did it
anyway.

I did a search
of your new wife
on the internet.

An art historian.

Ph. D. From Harvard,
book published at Yale.

Perfect for you
in every way.

And I was
very, very sorry.

Last Night

I dreamt
I was playing Ophelia
even though
I didn't know my lines.

Hamlet
had written out my part
in little books
he scattered about the stage.

We blocked the closing scene
twice.
Hamlet came in the door
home from work
tired and hungry

and I gave him a kiss.

Waking

I am dreaming....
I am dreaming, dreaming, dreaming....
Is that the radio? Is it time to get up?
I have to remember my dream....
I have to write a poem about it....

Up at 5.
Three cups of coffee.
Six cigarettes.
I can remember the feeling of the dream....

Wash and dry hair.
Put makeup on.
Get books together for class.
Only a fragment of the dream remains....

Toast cinnamon raisin bagel.
Drink orange juice.
Make lunch. Yogurt and crackers.

Leave! I think it was a good dream....
If only I could remember....

Drive to school.
Check bookstore schedule.
Arrive at Center for Independent Learning.
Banish the dream!
I've got work to do!

Wait. No students.

Write a poem?

It's all coming back to me now....
My dream was about you....

Working Girl

To Sylvia

When I first read your poems,
I knew exactly
what you were talking about.

My first boyfriend
Whom I thought was my true love
broke my heart
when he married someone else.

It was not until college
and my first breakdown
that I understood
The Bell Jar.

Somehow I knew all along
that it was waiting for me.

The Affair I Only
Dreamt About

I dreamt
about my high school boyfriend
last night.

He was married
and had four boys,
all grown up.

His wife
didn't care
if he had an affair
with me.

So my old lover and I
climbed into bed.

But the four boys
came home
and raided the refrigerator.
It was full of fried chicken.

I realized I hadn't had any dinner
but there was nothing left.

So my old lover and I
got back into bed.

But then I realized
that we were sleeping
in the lobby of a high-rise hotel.

That was enough for me.
I told his wife she could have him.

The Three Candles

(A PAINTING BY MARC CHAGALL)

Walking on air (just-
married) they *should* waltz across the
Sky. Flying

angels carry them
into the night
on a magic red carpet

of dreams. The
only touches of blue
find the church's steeple,

The beast from Shakespeare's
Dream, and the brand-new
dancing husband who

doesn't waltz but holds
his new wife from a
danger the angels

don't see. "Look out!"
cries from the villagers are
too late. Now the

bride, fallen angel,
spirals through time, a
sorrowful tune kept

by the violins.
Her husband weeps; his
music also ends.

Three lighted candles
burn; the highest
angel hopelessly

weeping holds out her
arms while the jester –
unquestioning – plays

his clarinet.

Back to School

Daddy brought
brand-new
64 Crayola Crayons
Paradise colored pencils
packs of wide-ruled notebook paper
home from the store
every fall.

He gave me
a small, red plastic pencil sharpener
to put inside
my clear plastic pencil case
which I snapped into my blue 3-ring binder.

When Daddy brought
orange Kingston pencils
home from work,
I sharpened them
watched each lead point emerge
from curls of wood,
imbibing the fragrance.

"Special Paint"

The salesman
proudly displayed
the Champagne edition VW Rabbit.

"You came back for it.
You're restored my faith in humanity,"
he remarked as he handed me the papers.

He went on, "You know,
this car has special paint."

I just smiled
as I signed the bill of sale.

Shift to a Baker's Square parking lot.

A man in a van
pulled out without looking
and hit my bumper.

My brand-new car.

Shift to the insurance adjuster.

"Oh my," he sighed, putting his hand
to his forehead.
"You know, this car has special paint."

"BZZZ"

My bumble bee alarm clock warns.
My subconscious swallows
The tail end of my dreams:
kittens playing with moonbeams
scrambled eggs served to prisoners of war....

I'm out of Folger's Breakfast Blend.
I'm out of peach nectar.
I'm out of Benson & Hedges menthol lights....

The glacial shower leaves me shivering.
My favorite powder-blue dress,
wrinkled in a sweaty heap,
sports strawberry stains
all down the front....

A helium sigh
escapes from my red balloon...
Then I remember,
"It's Saturday!"

Regrets

I have few regrets in life.
There are few episodes
I would change if I could.

But one incident
in particular
still makes me blush.

It was Halloween
and my sisters and I
were trick-or-treating.

One neighbor
an older lady
held out a plate of candy
and a Powerhouse bar
fell to the ground.

"I'll take it!"
I spouted immediately.

And then I saw it.
A box of candy corn.

How I coveted
that little box
with the candy corn inside.

I hoped no one would notice.

I put the Powerhouse bar
back on the plate
and took the candy corn.

Two Secret Gardens

It all began with two secret gardens.

Yours was in Germany,

and mine was in California.

Who'd have ever thought

we'd get this far?

We laughed about the movie,

Sixteen in Downers Grove,

and I cried

when we saw *Hoosiers* for ninety-nine cents

in College Park.

You see, we were destined to meet.

Germany isn't so far, really.

You were wearing your green Loden coat

and carrying your sewing machine

when you stepped onto the plane.

You came back with a husband. How will you come back this time?

My dream of California has died;

your dream of Germany is coming true.

I know this is good-bye.

Even here do we shake hands.

I always hoped

we would be best friends forever.

But, as you always say,

things always change.

I know you will not miss me.

You never seem to lack for company.

The beautiful tapestry suit you made me is still brand-new.
I will be wearing it long after
you have found your niche in Bonn.
I should have made you something in return.
I hope you will read the book I gave you,
and I hope you will write your novel.

I will never forget
our Labor Day trip to Philadelphia,
or was it New York?

Just kidding.
No matter what happens,
you always come up –
you will forgive me if I say it –
smelling like a rose.

It all began with two secret gardens.
Yours was in Germany,
and mine was in California.

I think I am cured
of dreaming about California.
Who'd have seen me through it
but you?
I wish you could still know me
in the happier times to come.

You don't have to dream about Germany any more.
Your dream, and your husband Reza's dreams,
are all coming true.

Germany isn't so far, really.
Maybe I will surprise you

and show up on your doorstep one day.
If I know your address.

We have been so close.
Who can gossip like you and I?
Your friendship has meant so much to me.
We always agree on the really important things,
like lace curtains.

You have changed me,
and you have changed my life.
Indiana, San Antonio, the army,
Edith Wharton, chips and dip –

How can we ever be strangers now?

Missing the Eighties

I met Rowena
in graduate school at the University of Maryland.

We went downtown to Washington, DC quite often.

To the Arena Stage theater
Where we saw *Measure for Measure*
and *Death of a Salesman,*

the Folger Shakespeare Library,
where I worked,

the Kennedy Center,
where we saw *The Heidi Chronicles,*

and the national Gallery of Art,
where we ate cream cheese sandwiches
on date nut bread
and saw "The White Girl."

We listened to an African-American radio station.
Every night at midnight, the DJ said, "Shoot for the moon!"

Rowena and I became close friends.
We liked Ruffles potato chips and French onion dip.
We had Halloween parties.
I wore white cardboard wings as Titania,
a gold lamé nightgown as Cleopatra
and a pink nightgown for Desdemona.

We missed KISS

We missed Fleetwood Mac

We Missed Blondie

We missed black leather and silver chains.

But we had beer and birthday cake.

We had lace curtains that we both liked.

We had a baby shower for Rowena and her husband.

Rowena and Reza moved to Africa.

I miss Rowena.

Moving Dreams

The movers are here
but I am still packing.

Half-empty boxes
litter the living room floor.

I grab a few books
and a glass jewelry box

that I know will break
and throw them in a carton.

I am not ready.
I have nowhere to go.

The Last Dance

The summer is so short.
It's after mid-July
and fall will soon be with us.
But for now,
Chelsea and I drink mango iced tea
in the fiery light of the sunset
and watch the magnolia tree dance.

Ludington, Michigan: A Childhood Memory

Blue-gray sand curled the round rubber toes of PF flyers, plaidflannel-lined corduroy whispers mingling with the circling gull cries. Hooded figures, one faded sweatshirt tomato-soup red for a blue-eyed smiling littleboy, padded the sloping shores.

Uncolored cottoncandy whitecaps, waterfloating swiftly, silently sought the hills of sand. Tagging the waves and each other, we four (ages 5, 9, 10, 12) stole the cold, damp air in big bites. Friendly waves washed our blue canvas feet, but gave no warm promise inviting us in.

A taller-than-I-am beachstick sandpoking walk turned up discovery in the sand: kingly black-and-white-bodied, scarlet-and-yellow-crest-beaked gulls rotting in time. Solemn-smiling religious weedflower-decked burial, adventure-sense and sympathy winning out over tears and maggoted rabbit-fur feathers was followed by mothertype "youdidnttouch those germy birds no mama," pitterpat back behind gray sandwalls to clandestinely cover and flower and tearstain more riddled, bacteria-beautiful corpses.

Breeze-ruffled lavender flowers in place, we sombered down the sandandes, raising our elbows now and then, while shimmery-scarfed mother wavered and smiled a ruby-mouthed come-along.

We left pockmarks in the periwinkle-velvet sand, tracking the breakwater. "Mama, you mean it breaks the water? How does it do that, Mommy?" Beige cement sun-bleached arm reaching into the blue water, wide brown breadth seeming much narrower. Our shoelaces touched the many-shaded cement, so very near the water, and so very far from shore, and yet not wet.

A steamship-ferry raced us to the lighthouse-finish. We lost, and waved and halloed the winner-ship, which didn't stop.

We had left giggling Daddy with his camera in the film-change dark to skip flat, gray smoothstones across the wrinkles in the lake. We met him and son, stones in hand, at the edge of the sand and the water's edge and they skilled us with their talents.

Listening to the surf and following its feet, we found heavy, pitted driftwood holding up from the sand a thousand or more ladybugs. Clean and alive, their eyelashes tangled, they made their home and lived by the sea.

The picnic-dinner state parks were calling us and our tired car as the sun burned down and we drove out of sight. Our white-stockinged seashell feet and clean, dry hands said "Good-bye" to the ladybugs as the evening blanket settled about the shoulders of the lake.

Kiki and Ed

Kiki, the impish blonde
the live wire
the actress
the life of the party.

Ed, the Shakespearean king
quiet
but quick with smiles
and laughter.

Together you directed countless productions:

Arsenic and Old Lace
A Midsummer Night's Dream
Beyond the Fringe
She Stoops to Conquer
A Funny Thing Happened on the Way to the Forum
Tartuffe
Anne Frank

You spoiled me
with the best parts I would ever play:
Titania, Elmire.

Some said you were perfectionists
too hard on the actors
but I thought
you were just perfect.

I had no idea
how valuable
my theater experience
would be in the future –
I thought
I was just having fun.

Thank you
for the example of your true love
which grew with each play
deeper, lovelier
overflowing like a waterfall.

In Her Shoes

She gave me the movie for Christmas.
"Don't read anything into it," she warned.

But I did read something into it.

It was our relationship:

a struggling actress
and a struggling lawyer

clawing at each other
at times

but in the end

friends
rivals
sisters.

The Bride

She was forty-five minutes late.
My friend, the groom,
was starting to fidget.

But she did come –
young, petite, and blonde
with a long, white train.

The Mass was long.

The reception went quickly.

Someone put an apron
over the bride's gown
and her father sang her a song.

The time came
for the bride and groom to leave,
and the bride was in tears.
she couldn't say good-bye
to her parents.

My friend, the groom,
started to fidget.

A few years later,
they sent me a Christmas card.

My friend, the groom,
had a good, steady job.

He had built them a house

all by himself.

They had two small children.

There was a picture of the bride
and she was smiling.

The Tornado

Waking up
groggily
to the sound of the radio:
"Joplin, Missouri....
hundreds of fatalities...."

Becky!
My dear friend
from graduate school,
her husband,
and their two girls
all live in Joplin.

I reach for the phone
but think
"No, I'll wait a few days."

Three days go by.
Dear Becky
her mischievous smile
reddish-brown hair and freckles
cute enough to be Tom Sawyer's girl.

Dear Becky
poet and Milton scholar
former professor
world traveler

Did the wind
pick up her house

twirl it around
and land it in Kansas?

I finally call.

"Is Becky there?"

I couldn't understand
the answer at first
but then
her voice came over the wire.

The tornado
had passed by
four blocks from their home.

Twelve miles of destruction.

The largest tornado
ever recorded.

"Becky, how ARE you?"

"Fine. How are YOU?"

Part-time Ghosts

I remember
looking at ashes
on the upholstery
in other people's cars.
"When I have a car," I said to myself,
"I'll make sure there are no ashes."

I remember
looking at a lonely restaurant customer
who had only pie and coffee.

"How pitiful," I said to myself.
"I hope I am never that pitiful."

I remember
looking at mature women
who wore open-toed shoes
"Who wants to look at those old toes?"
I said to myself.

I remember
the part-time ghosts, nomads,
who wandered the halls, afraid,
and never published anything.
"If that happens to me," I swore,
'I will quit and do something else."

Now a part-time ghost myself,
With ashes in my car,
I consider pie and coffee a treat.
Who wants to look at these old feet?

Good Luck

I went to pay my car insurance
on a snowy day.

My agent
has her office
in a cute little brick house
on a steep hill.

I park in the lot
and make my way up the hill
to the back door.

"Here, let me help you,"
a young woman offers.

I object,
but she takes my hand
and helps me up
to the steps.
I must be an old lady.

I pay my bill
and go out the way I came in.

The young woman is gone.

I look balefully
at the hill.
Going down looks dicey.

I try,
and find myself
running, sliding, running, sliding
down the icy hill
on the soles of my shoes
flapping my arms
like a bird that has forgotten how to fly

All the way to my parked car.

But I do not fall.

Goodwill

Four pillowcases
packed with new and used clothing.

I put them in the back seat.

Driving to Goodwill,
I feel cheerful and purposeful.

I open the car window to let the wind blow
and sing along with the radio.

When I get to the store,
there are two other blonde ladies
with several overflowing plastic bags.

We smile at each other.
I feel good about myself.

We are all three surprised
by a strong young man
wheeling a cart
out to the parking lot for us.

"Wow," I think. "He's really nice."

Blew me out of the park.

"The Quickest Promise Home"

HOMAGE TO DORIS MOZER

Her first husband
sold chewing gum
and wore pointy shoes.
She chewed gum
and sharpened shoes.

But what she really wanted
were violets.

Her second husband
was a writer.
She chewed the fat
and sharpened pencils.

But what she really wanted
were violets.

Her third husband passed on.
The children now grown,
she started a garden
where she grew
violet, violets,
and more
violets.

Omega

The hustle-bustle surrounds us.
Waiters and waitresses
in black and white
bend over filled tables.

The waiter pours us each some coffee.
Regular for me, decaf for Marta.

Marta eats half
of her cherry Kijafa crepes
and I eat half of my eggs.

The eggs are over hard,
just the way I like them,
with ham, mushrooms, hash brown potatoes,
and blended cheese.

We eye the ice cream fountain
but are too full to indulge.

One more cup of coffee
and we are out the door
leaving the hustle-bustle
for the quiet of Barnes & Noble bookstore.

Mamma Mia

The newspaper reviews
were kind of negative.
"Pace too frenetic,
two stars."

But I loved the musical
All's Well That Ends Well,
and they panned that, too.

I'm not all that much
of an ABBA fan,
but "Dancing Queen,"
always makes me smile.

And, besides,
I'm a sucker for musicals.

The Other Movie

The air is cool
in the movie theater.

Butter and popcorn
Junior Mints
Raisinets
litter the floor.

Teenagers
sweep the carpet
and disappear
behind a secret door.,

The movie is over.
Streams of young men,
long-haired, unshaven,
wearing brash T-shirts
and sagging jeans
pass by us.

It must have been
Batman, The Dark Knight.

Coming Home

Halsted Street.
Still in the city.
Chicago.
The city of skyscrapers
that look like stereos.
Rush hour traffic.
Got to get home.

Racine.
I get on the Eisenhower,
tense and tired from my day.
I am making lists in my head.
Have to grade papers,
have to plan lessons for tomorrow.

Ashland and Paulina.
Bumper-to-bumper.
I check my watch.
Probably fifty minutes to go.

Sacramento.
Don't I wish.
The air shimmers with the heat.
The line of cars
stretches as far as I can see.

Independence.
What a pipe dream.
The afternoon sun
is shining right in my eyes.
The traffic is stop-and-go.

Harlem Avenue.
It won't be long now.
I step on the accelerator,
and the cars space themselves out.

I ease into the curve at Hillside –
The Strangler.
Left lane, Roosevelt Road.
The home stretch.

The gray sky
gives way to turquoise blue
with white cumulus.

Everywhere green,
green grass,
green trees,
green, green, green.

Meyers Road.
The big pond
shaded by willow trees.

Butterfield Road.
The mansions
hidden from the street
by leafy maples and elms.

Fairview Avenue.
Gierz Street.

Home.

I am relaxing on the deck
sipping raspberry iced tea.

Cruise, Part One

A perfect day.
Sunny, warm, 80 degrees.

The boat was huge:
eight hundred people.

I could feel the gentle pull
of the boat through the water.

I got a little nervous
when we sailed past the breakwater.

The Chicago skyline
retreated to the horizon.

Pleasure boats passed us
and the people waved.

We started to turn a little
and I realized

we were still in sight
of Navy Pier.

Cruise, Part Two

blue-green, blue-green

white

blue-green

The baby-blue sky

arches over

the rippling teal-blue lake.

White sails

float haphazardly.

We move

slowly, gently,

tippling

through the calm waves.

Wendy's Poems

Wendy has the wanderlust.
Her adventures soon turn into poems:
San Miguel, Green Lake, Washington DC.

But my favorites are closer to home.
A midnight conversation between her sleepy mom and dad:
"Come to bed."
"I have to find my teeth...."
"Come to bed."

A cosmic wedding ring from an astronomer husband
and honeymoon horseback riding.
She recalled the wind in her hair;
he the sweat and the flies.

A funny, poignant moment
finding pink panties at the curb
and checking to make sure
they weren't hers.

Secrets overheard at the China Chef
and the wisdom of naughty Uncle Norman.

Write more poems, Wendy.
Write more touching and tender poems.

Whose pink underpants
were those, anyway?

Through the Window

The sun is peeking through the clouds.
I feel its warmth
through the glass window
where I am sitting at McDonald's.

A minivan pulls by
fresh out of the drive-thru.
Inside is a woman
with two swirly vanilla ice cream cones.

She hands one
to the child in the back seat
wraps her mouth around the other one
and drives on.

The dark gray clouds
slowly cover the sun
and I feel the cold air
through the window.

A Bargain at the Price

It was my first business venture,
other than selling Girl Scout cookies.

I had it all figured out.
I would put penny candy in baggies
and sell it.

Strawberry whips, Bazooka bubble gum,
"Bike" banana caramels, Tootsie rolls,
black licorice wound around a jawbreaker,
a candy "record."

I had a brilliant thought:
Why not put ten cents' worth of candy
in each bag,
and charge five cents?

A real bargain.

I tied each baggie
with a hopeful red ribbon.

All afternoon
I sat at a card table
with a sign, "Candy, five cents."

I didn't sell a one.

I must have been
destined to be a poet.

Starry, Starry Night

I was lucky to have the job.

Personnel Records clerk at a security guard company.

Caren, my best friend,
got me the job.
Her father was the president,
and his friend, Mr. Reavely,
was the chairman of the board.

Mr. Reavely smoked cigars.
He poked around the office every day
to make sure we were all working.

I didn't want to go to the company picnic
but Caren and I both went.
At the Foxy Lady Ranch
way out in Plano, Illinois.

Mr. Reavely wore a chef's hat
and flipped the steaks.
"How do you want yours, Barb?"
I was floored.
I didn't think he even knew my name.

I did not win the potato sack race
but it was fun.

I did win the rolling pin throwing contest.
My prize: a set of kitchen utensils.

In spite of myself
I had a good time
and best of all
were the stars
that covered the sky
on that starry, starry night.

The Pet Parade

At the Pet Parade
my childhood came back to me:
1962.
Patty, Annalisa, and I
sitting on the curb
wearing pointed Chinese hats
and sunglasses with little guns on them.
Ali Baba and the forty thieves
threw us sugar candy
and the street cleaners
swept up the confetti.

Summer Coming

It's been a long, warm spring –
rare for Chicago.
Usually we go straight from winter
Into summer heat.

But this year
temperate days
follow temperate days
warm enough to be pleasant,
cool enough to get things done.

The summer stretches out before us.
We have plans:
teaching, writing,
poetry club meetings,
volunteering at a Shakespeare festival,
poems, poems, poems....

Slipping

The day is slipping away....

I got up early
with a list of things to do
and I let the day
get away from me.

The summer is slipping away....

Fourth of July is past,
the fall clothes are in the stores,
time to start back-to-school.

I let the summer
get away from me....

My life is slipping away....

Silver Skipper of Gostyn

I

We called him "Skippy."

When we brought him home
a toy poodle puppy
he tried to jump up on the couch with us.

When he realized
that his little paws
couldn't reach the top
he deflated like a little silver balloon.

We laughed
And picked him up.

Normally the couch was off-limits.

We taught him every trick
we could think of:
sit, speak, stay, come,
sit up, shake hands, jump, dance...
He mastered them all.

If we said "Roll over,"
he would do every trick he knew,
and then, if we insisted,
he would roll over, too.

He didn't like to "roll over."

III

He loved the Christmas tree.
The glass ornaments,
the lights,
and the presents.

One year we wrapped up
a new ball for Skippy.

Early Christmas morning
He opened it
and was playing with it
when we found him.

Nothing else under the tree was touched.

How did he know that ball was for him?

IV

Once
I was sitting on the floor
feeling sorry for myself
and Skippy
gently nosed my hand
so I would pet his back.

He was so solemn and so tender
I knew I loved that dog
and he loved me, too.

Doggy Dream

"Puppies for sale!
Three for $5."

But I can only have one.

I choose a little yellow Lab,
and tentatively
reach out to pet him

as a big, black poodle
jumps into my lap
and licks my face.

Cats

We are cozy, we are comfy
at Chelsea's kitchen table,
drinking decaf out of cat mugs,
eating fudge stripe cookies
out of a cat plate.

The sunset
casts a yellow glow
around us.

Mink, the fluffy chocolate brown Persian,
is eating Meow Mix.

The African violet
is in full bloom.

Spring Rain

Chelsea and I
sit outside
at the café table
at Starbucks
leisurely drinking good coffee
having good conversation.

We plan a girls'
night out:
organizing our wardrobes
coloring our hair blonde
painting our fingernails red
eating pizza and drinking beer
having good conversation.

My aunt is moving in
with her boyfriend on June 10th.
Chelsea's friend Darla
Is getting married on June 11th.
Chelsea and Bob's second anniversary
Is on June 15th.

It's spring.
It threatens rain
but it's not raining yet.

Coffee House

A moth
beats its wings
against the window
which has a neon sign:
espresso
latte
mocha
cappuccino.

Chelsea and I
are writing poems.

Everyone else
is glued to the TV.

They are watching the new movie,
Flight 93.

The importance of poems
pales
as I remember 9/11.

When I look again for the moth,
it is gone.

Ariel

amazing
misty
ariogirl
with limpid cocker spaniel eyes
filled with Bradbury skies
and
a milkmaid's mouth.

hands like slender asterisks
with daisies on her fingertips
through butterfly lashes
she cries opal tears
that fall silently
into the quiet deep wishing-well
of her soul.

Sonnet 1
after William Shakespeare

From fairest creatures we desire increase
that thereby beauty's rose might never die;
in reproduction some find inner peace,
eternal life – but, I'm afraid, not I.

When I was young, I feared the pangs of birth,
an early death, and, most of all, myself.
You catch my drift. And, sadly, what on earth
would I do with a child? A changeling elf?

So as I gravely counsel you, my dear,
ponder your heart,m search deep within your soul.
I may regret my choice each passing year;
It may be that a child would make you whole.

You are the only one who can decide.
Whatever happens, I am on your side.

Sonnet 2
after William Shakespeare

When forty winters shall besiege thy brow,
and dig deep trenches in thy beauty's field,
when thou art not so lovely and beloved as now,
perhaps when both of us have nearly healed,

what will you do to make your life worthwhile?
You may not be so happy then as now.
What sports, games, and delights will make you smile?
Perhaps you will be happier then than now.

Neither of us have the eternal life
bestowed by children. Therefore, we must strive
by other means to win eternal life.
How may we daily know we are alive?

Sir Philip Sidney had the answer right:
his Astrophel said, "Look in thy heart and write."

Sonnet 30
after William Shakespeare

When to the sessions of sweet silent thought
I summon up remembrance of things past,
the things I've tried to do that came to nought,
the things retained, that were not meant to last,
I think on thee, dear friend, my dearest love,
my one misdeed, my thirty-year mistake,
my many misperceptions, and, my love,
my trials of your patience. For my sake,

my dearest sweet, forget you knew me when
all innocence, I thought our love was true.
Forget I promised to be friends, and then
forget me, even if I plead with you
one more appeal, for I already know
the verdict is that I should let you go.

Sonnet 42
after William Shakespeare

That thou hast her it is not all my grief,
and yet it may be said I loved her dearly;
that she hath thee is of my wailing chief,
a loss in love that touches me more nearly.

Best friends for thirty years, she and I must part.
I defended her when others called her false,
never guessing that she might steal your heart,
that you and she might join to play me false.

Beautiful she is, and accomplished, too.
Her dark eyes complement her darker soul.
Once before she took a love who was not true,
a love I needed to make my heart whole.

I suppose everyone has their secret vice,
and hers is that she has betrayed me twice.

Sonnet 117
after William Shakespeare

Accuse me thus, and I will answer thee,
say I have loved too much, and loved too long,
one who does not remember me.
Accuse me thus, and I will answer in song:

I have loved too much, and loved too long,
one who does not remember me.
You married elsewhere, and that makes me wrong
to carry a torch, to try to make you love me.

So, I have loved too much and loved too long,
one who does not remember me.
I have learned that sometimes love can be too strong.
I have learned I cannot make you love me.

I have spent thirty years thus mistaking;
To tell the truth, it was a fault worth making.

To My

Shakespeare

Professor

How to be a Great Writer: My Foolproof Method

Be born in 1564.

Seduce a local girl and get caught.

Marry her.

Have a daughter six months later.

Have twins.

Move to London and get a job

holding horses' reins

outside a theater.

Pretend to have an affair with Queen Elizabeth I.

Write about it.

Narrowly escape getting your right hand cur off.

Put on a play every day.

Write 37 plays, 2 narrative poems,

and 154 sonnets.

Have friends who will publish your work

after you die.

To My Chaucer Professor

Everyone in your class
had to memorize and perform
the first thirty lines
of *The Canterbury Tales.*

We read Chaucer
without a glossary.
It was
incomprehensible.

I was young, twenty-two.
You must have been fifty.

In your black suit
you looked like a funeral director.

You left notes –
invitations –
in my mailbox.

I didn't know what to do.

You were married,
with children.
You were old,
I was young.

I had a boyfriend.

      * * *

You gave me a "C" in your class.

In graduate school,
a "C" is a failing grade.

I went to talk to you about the grade.

You shut the door.

I reached out my hand to shake yours.
"No hard feelings...."
but
you drew me near
and bellowed, "Kiss me!"

Obedient as a child,
I kissed your wrinkled cheek.

You planted a passionate French kiss on my mouth
and your hands began to stray all over my body.

Startled,
I stepped lightly back.
"I just remembered," I stated evenly,
"I have a student in my office."

I got away
as I had never before
gotten away
from my grandfather.

　　　　* * *

It's the first day of spring
and I am eating vanilla ice cream
out in the mild, damp air.

I can still recite
the first thirty lines
of *The Canterbury Tales,*
but I don't know why.

First Memory

We have a photo
of the four of us kids together.

The three girls
in a circle
around little Benjamin
the only boy.

I remember
looking at the photographer
and thinking,
"I want to look sexy
like Mama
for the picture."

I shook my blonde hair
and ran my hands
along my black velvet jumper.

I lowered my lip
and looked dead into the camera.

My Career as a Ballerina

I wanted to be a ballerina.
When we went to my grama's house
we would watch their color TV.

If there was music
I would dance.
Twirl, jump, twirl some more.

Grampa would say,
"Sit down!
I can't get a good view
Of the TV."

"Listen to Me"

The nurse
held out the syringe.
I was five.
I hated shots.
I was left-handed
and the needle
was headed
for my left arm.

"Wait a minute,"
I wanted to explain.
"I'm left-handed!"

But the words stuck
in my five-year-old mouth.

"Waitaminute, waitaminute,
Waitaminute...."

She gave me the shot
in my left arm.

II

Tobey was a college friend
my freshman year.

Tobey, Tommy, and me.
We were a trio.

We were hanging around
in my dorm room

and somehow

Tobey got me on the floor
and sat on my stomach
his knees on either side
of my hips.

"What is he doing?
Am I still a virgin?"

I screamed. He didn't move.
I was pinned to the floor.
I screamed again.

Tobey got mad at me
for screaming.

III

My violin lesson was on Saturday mornings.
Grampa was taking me this week.

I knew what that meant.

Instead of going to the music store
we would go to the golf course.

Grampa would park in a secluded spot
and then it would begin:

"Please don't, Grampa.
Grampa, please stop...."

"I don't like it, Grampa.
Grampa, please don't...."

It never made any difference.

Patience

My grandfather taught me patience
in the living room
while everyone else
read the Sunday paper,
in the family room
while everyone else
watched TV,
in the bathroom with no lock
locked in the car with no key.

II

I sweep and mop the wood floor.
Tears fall.
I dust the glass-topped tables.
Tears make little circles on the glass.

I vacuum the beige rug.
No one can hear me,
so the sobs start.

It is 9:30 P.M.
I have twenty-five papers to grade before 6:30 A.M.
Each paper takes half an hour.

I polish the cherry wood cabinet
and dining room chairs.

We are having a party tomorrow.

The Chinese Dragon in my Minds Eye

In my mind's eye
I see a little girl
locked in a car
in a secluded spot
on a golf course.

She kneels in the front seat
looking out the back window.
Her arms
rest on top of the front seat.

Her underpants
are pulled down
around her knees.
Her bottom is cold.

As is his long-standing custom,
her grandfather
repeatedly
violates her
with his middle finger.

The little girl
frozen in place
is silent.

She can feel
his finger

inside her.

She does not cry any more.
She has given up
begging him to stop
because he never stops.

She wants so badly
to be somewhere else
anywhere else.

Her mind
detaches
from her body
rises slowly
and soon
she is far, far away.

PART II

In my mind's eye
I am Atalanta
not running a footrace
but climbing a glass mountain.

My path is steep
and slippery,
and golden apples
are strewn in my way.

I fall many times
taking one step forward
and two steps back.

Up at the mountain's top
through white clouds
I can see
My favorite teachers:
Miss Rotsko, Maggie, and Jane McDonald.

Miss Rotsko
my second grade teacher
published my first poem.

She was always careful to remind us
that she was Russian,
White Russian.

When I told her
I had decided to be a poet
she wisely advised me
to make sure
I had something to fall back on.

She once told me
that if some of my B's
didn't turn into A's
they might sting me.

Miss Rotsko
was the first teacher
to mention Shakespeare to me.

She said he was a great poet
and I should read his poems someday.

Maggie
or Mrs. Cantrall
as I called her

before we became friends,
was my English teacher
my senior year of high school.

I always thought of her
as the glorious woman
on the prow
of the English Department ship.

Maggie
held Book Club meetings
in her own home,
and published the literary magazine,
The Muse.
She wrote poems herself, too.

Maggie
sent three of my poems
To the IATE: Illinois Association of Teachers of English.
I received an honorable mention
and she presented the award to me
at my senior honors assembly.

Many years later,
we became very dear friends.

Jane McDonald
my dissertation director
was the second person
to show me
that love
and education
are the same thing.

She glowed with spiritual love
like a saint.

Through the white clouds
I can see
Miss Rotsko, Maggie, and Jane
at the glass mountain's peak
but they can't see me.

What would they say
if they could see me
here
in my predicament?

Where is my hero,
My Superman, my Supergirl?
My Renaissance man
has led me
over the edge of a cliff
and I am just
another lemming.

Seclusion

I wake at 4:00 A.M.
I have not really slept.
There are two chairs
at the foot of my bed.
The nurses watched me all night.
Suicide watch.

I refused to take off my clothes.
I argued with the scale
about my weight.
I refused to allow the nurses
to take my blood.

I was feeling mean.

I paced up and down
near the nurses' station.
The plastic cups
for urine samples
were all lined up
on the counter.
A male nurse
gave me a pleading look
so I took the cup
with my name on it.

Laugh, laugh.

I know the nurses
laugh at the patients.

Laugh at us
behind our backs.
You think it's funny?

My grandfather
raped me with his finger
countless times.

You think it's funny?

I closed the bathroom door
and forgot about the plastic cup.

When I opened the door,
there were four orderlies
just hanging around.

I asked, no one in particular,
"What? No gold record?"
and the orderlies jumped me.

I knew what that meant.

I relaxed my body,
offering no resistance,
but began to spout:
"Men are all criminals,
Rapists, buttfuckers, criminals.
You're going to give me
A shot in the butt?
What year is this?
For God's sake, it's 1999!
Go ahead,
I've got a cute butt."

They gave me a shot
and took my blood.
I threw my glasses
to the nurse who asked for them
and the frames broke.

Compassion

I know why
emaciated young girls refuse to eat.

I know why
psychiatric patients cut themselves.

I know why
Emily Dickinson
published only seven poems
in her lifetime.

I know why
J.D. Salinger
never published another book
after *Catcher in the Rye.*

I know why
Sylvia Plath
put her head in the oven.

I know why
my father's workbench
was left in a complete mess
when he passed away.

I know why
my mother
made four little pairs
of brown suede Indian moccasins
while she was in the hospital.

And I understand.

What I Told Dr. Mahomet

She asked me about December 1999.
I was working at Service Merchandise
in the jewelry department.

I remember Christmas Eve.
I finished paying for the diamond ring.
I was last in line.
There were two young men ahead of me.

I knew the clerk He was an orphan.
He told me
to wear the wedding band
inside the diamond ring
because that was closest
to my heart.

What I Told Dr. Mahomet

PART II: PATTY'S WEDDING

I didn't really have the money
or the time
to go to my own sister's wedding.
My younger sister.

The invitation had a quote
from *West Side Story:*
"Tonight, tonight,
won't be just any night...."
I wanted to go.

So I put it on a new credit card.

I remember I carried my own suitcases
and took public transportation
to Washington International Airport.
I had to get up at 5 A.M.
The plane was supposed to leave at 8 A.M.,
but we were delayed.
Something about an engine part?

The plane was full of eighth graders
on their way home
from their graduation
trip to Washington, D.C.

We waited for hours.

It was hot, humid, and close.

The natives were restless.

The captain told us
to get something to eat.
I remember I had a sandwich
at the "Love of Life" café.

They couldn't find the part,
so they switched us to another plane
that had a layover in Denver.

In Denver,
I had a drink
with a Scandinavian girl
who was studying to be an airline pilot.

That was where the airline
lost my luggage,
in Denver.

The shoes I had planned to wear
to Patty's wedding
were lost.

I didn't get to San Francisco
until 1 A.M. California time.
The first thing I saw
was a monitor
with all "Santa Barbara" flights
listed for the next day.
Gladys. a friend,
was supposed to pick me up
at the baggage claim.

But she wasn't there. I waited and waited.
The airport was empty.

Then I heard my name
over the loudspeaker.

I was supposed to walk out
the automatic door.

Gladys picked me up at the curb.
I guess she didn't want to pay
for parking.

We arrived at her house
after 2 A.M.,
twenty-plus hours after
I had left Washington.
I wanted to go straight to bed,
but I thought
I should call my brother
to let him know I had arrived.
The phone rang and rang.
He finally picked up,
and his first words were,
"Gee, you sound grumpy."

What I Told Dr. Mahomet

PART III: WHAT HAPPENED AT THE OAKS

I was alone in the room
with the doctor.

He told me to take off my blouse.

I wondered why a psychiatrist
wanted to look at my breasts
but I did what he said.

Betrayal

My best friend
for over thirty years,
she had betrayed my trust
once before
by "stealing" a boy I liked
in high school.

The boy she "borrowed"
was lent to us
for only a short time:
he was hit by a train
and killed
at the age of eighteen.

Her loss was great.

Small wonder, then,
That I didn't
invite her
to go to California with me
to visit someone
who intrigued me.

I always regarded her
As a sort of older sister,
a confidante.
But I confided too much.

She gave me a framed picture
of a blindfolded girl
playing the harp.

I knew I was blind,
blind to her
blind to him
but, try as I might,
I just couldn't see.

One sentence
and I knew
she had betrayed me
again.

"I wanted to be Titania," she confessed,
and the way she said it,
and the way she looked at
my diamond ring,
I knew she had "borrowed"
someone I didn't care to lend.

"Everything is temporary,"
I answered quickly,
appropriating one of her favorite lines.
"Even best friends."

I flounced out of my chair
as I finished my sentence
and stuck her with the check.

The tears came later.

 Timidity

I am too timid....I am not assertive enough....."Don't let people shit all over you; open your mouth!"

I believe it is futile for me to assert myself...People just shoot me down....I get angry and give up....

Why am I sucked into abusive relationships? Why do I put up with abuse?

Why can't I defend myself?

Why don't people back down and allow me the luxury of my own opinions and my own feelings?

Why do I sweep my feelings under the rug until I can't take it anymore?

I am confused and exhausted....Cecy is right....My thoughts are bouncing around in my head like lottery ping-pong balls....

Thank God I am not psychotic....

"Not Funny," Part I

I told Renata, a youthful fellow student
in a Renaissance literature class
that I had a delusion
that I was Emma Woodhouse.

We laughed about it together.
I told her
I had a very rich fantasy life.

It was funny.

The next day, the class met again,
and Renata stayed after
to talk to the professor.
So did I.

"Do you know what Barbara told me?"
she asked him, laughing.

"Don't tell him," I interrupted,
and she fell silent.
It wasn't funny any more.

"Not Funny," Part II

I told Jane, my dissertation director,
an amusing story
I uncovered in my research:
a Shakespearean actress, Miss Bride,
had to abandon her part of Imogen
because she was great with child
and couldn't fit into her doublet and hose.

We laughed about it together.

We laughed again
when she learned
she was expecting her second child.

But when my article about
Miss Bride was published,
and I had my thirteenth nervous breakdown
and Professor S. was dying of cancer,
I decided to finish my dissertation at home.

It wasn't funny anymore.

I was reminded
of the only time
I thought I might be pregnant.

I wanted the child
because it was yours.

As it turned out,
I wasn't pregnant,
and it wasn't funny at all.

The Silent Woman

A RESPONSE TO "SPEAK OUT," BY PATRICIA E. POPE

"An angry woman
Is like a troubled fountain...."
Men express anger freely.
Women – almost never.

Even good Queen Bess,
who tried to make England
a paradise for women,
encouraging literacy and education,
was often forced to apologize for her sex.

It took all her wit
to outsmart her Parliament,
who insisted she marry
and produce an heir.

Instead, she made marriage negotiations
her foreign policy
ultimately eluding
the many would-be husbands
who ought only to rule her
and her kingdom.

She played many false
in order to be true
to her secret beloved,
who was married to another.

After her death,
a whole generation of Jacobean dramatists
penned some of the most hate-filled
antifeminist literature
ever written.

Even today,
over four hundred years later,
many male professors
are blind to the vitriol
female professors
are too polite to mention.

Watches

You keep perfect time
dependable as a metronome.
You won't be hurried,
Your heart never skips a beat.
No flights of fancy
just tick, tick, tick....

You watch over me
a father's vigilant regard
steadying my moods
always ready with a joke
or a story.

You keep me on course....
Tick, tick, tick....

A Golden Shovel Poem:
a dialogue between
Titania and Oberon

"LOVE LOOKS NOT WITH THE EYES
BUT WITH THE MIND."

T: "What cheer, my love? Is not our love true **love**?
What would I not do for one of your sweet **looks**?
Give thee the boy?" O: "Love me or love me **not**,
give me the changeling child and I'll go **with**
thee." T: "The spring, the summer, childing autumn, **the**
angry winter, the mazed world." O: "Her **eyes**
are streaked with love-in-idleness. Now **but**
to the Athenians. Gentle Puck, go **with**
the purple flower, engender so **the**
thing of great constancy, love of the **mind.**"

A Golden Shovel Poem: Twelfth Night: Viola and Orsino

"This girl that loves you, my lord, must not **she**
be answered? A blank, my lord?" Orsino **sat,**
rapt. The music had a dying fall, **like**
the world ending. "My lord, surely **Patience**
must be a virtue. Have you sent me **on**
a Fool's errand? Must I bear it as **a**
man? My love, I will build a **monument**
for you in pretty verse and keep **smiling,**
giving the world something to wonder **at."**
"She sat like Patience on a monument, smiling at **grief."**

A Golden Shovel Poem:
As You Like It: Rosalind,
disguised as Ganymede, to Phebe

"I'll tell you in your ear when's best to **sell.**
Buy low, sell high. Then you will know, **when**
you sell whatever you want to sell, that **you**
have made the best deal you possibly **can.**
Of course, the fewer things, the more that **you**
can charge. Conversely, more things **are**
worth less apiece. Supply and demand. **Not**
fair, perhaps, but the law of the land. **For**
you, the rule is different. I'll tell you **all:**
Sell when you can, you are not for all **markets."**

A Golden Shovel Poem: Twelfth Night: Viola, disguised as Cesario

"Orsino, Olivia, and me. **O,**
my love is as hungry as the sea. O, **Time,**
thou teach'st me patience. Hourly I learn, **thou**
see'st, but I cannot, travails I **must**
accomplish. Somehow, too, I must **untangle**
this wanton's wanton glance. In all of **this,**
I serve the absent Duke, who loves me **not.**"
"O, Time, thou must untangle this, not **I.**
It is too hard a knot for me t'untie."

A Golden Shovel Poem: from Antony and Cleopatra: Cleopatra

"I'll set a bourn how far to be beloved."

"If I lose myself in you, my love, **I'll**
no longer be Queen of Egypt. You **set**
quite a difficult problem for me, **a**
'no-win' situation. I need a **bourn**
to protect myself. How I have loved, **how**
I have lost in the past. Love me as **far**
as you wish, but please understand, not **to**
complain, I know when Fulvia calls, she must **be**
answered. Can you dispel my fears, my **beloved?**"

A Snake Poem: from A Midsummer Night's Dream

"THE POET'S PEN...GIVES TO AIRY NOTHING A LOCAL HABITATION AND A NAME."

The first thing a magician learns is that
there is no magic....The **poet's** lesson,
a similar one, concerns her perfumed **pen.**
It is not ink, paper, nor pen which **gives**
the poet her special magic. "**To** sleep,
perchance to dream," "we're **airy** spirits all."
The will o'th'wisp is something/**nothing;**
the paradox **a** poet's provenance. The
local bricklayer's advice: to write
a living line, sweat blood. **Habitation**
and home hath she none, save Mount Helicon.
The critic roars, "Would she had blotted **a**
thousand!" Woman scribbler, a poet's **name.**

How do I love thee? Part I

How do I love thee? Let me count the ways:
I truly love your energetic walk,
your fragrant pipe smoke and your deep blue eyes.
I even love the thoughtful way you talk.
I love the freedom I have in loving you.
I love my life, my dream, what I profess.
I love your gritty sense of humor, too.
But I must also honestly confess,
I never wanted to be a June bride,
blushing and shy. I guess I was too wild.
And I never wanted to settle down
with a real day job. I guess I was too wild.
In truth, I have only one regret:
we should have had a child.

How do I love thee? Part II

How do I love thee? Let me count the ways:
I love you and your energetic walk
The way you outshine all my highest praise.
I even love the thoughtful way you talk.
I love my life, my freedom, and my call.
But if you were to ask me to come back,
I'd leave it in an instant, leave it all,
even if my job were tenure-track.
I love the energy I steal from you.
I love to read your science fiction books.
How can I help it if I've lost my looks?
I don't know what I'll do if you retire.
I'll have to print the poems you inspire.

The Sunne Rising

Is the sun setting or rising?

I am backwards and inside-out
but I know what a double star is,
it is two children
making angels in the snow.

I am a ballerina after all
but I have forgotten the answer
to the whole puzzle:
I brush my teeth wrong,
I sleep on the wrong side of the bed,
I even eat wrong.

The Redcrosse Knight forgives Una, doesn't he?
Orsino always chooses Viola, doesn't he?
Doesn't Leontes always forgive Hermione?
Does Posthumus always forgive Imogen?

I will wait for you....
If it takes forever
I will wait for you....

Catherine Deneuve made a mistake.
She should have waited forever.

If I were Catherine,
I would wait forever for you.

But I am a little sparrow,
I am Edith Piaf,

"Je ne regrette rien...."
"There is special Providence in the fall of a sparrow...."
I think I have become you,
my dear Hamlet....

Lady Catherine de Bourgh
tests Lizzy to read her mind
to see if her love is true
to see if her heart is pure.

Lizzy loved Mr. Darcy from the beginning.

He hurt her feelings.
She was afraid of him.

He said she was too proud.
He said she wasn't a pretty girl.

Lizzy doesn't get a lot of winks.

Mr. Darcy make it impossible
for Lizzy to say "yes."

Mr. Darcy has a touch of Don Juan in him,
but Mr. Darcy has a pure heart.

Mr. Darcy tricks Elizabeth Bennett in a good way.

She finally figures it out;
he loved her all along.

Only then does she reveal
that she loved him all along, too.

Romeo and Juliet
magically transform
into Beatrice and Benedick.

Their story
is a love story
with a happy ending
after all.

Psalm

I was afraid I had forgotten you,
my love, it has been so long.
Will I recognize your face?
I have suffered in my loneliness
more than I can say.
The truth is I have forgotten myself,
I have forgotten my own life.
Please, my dearest love,
help me to remember.
Let us meet face-to-face.
In remembering you,
I will remember my own soul.

Vacation

A tropical splash
on the shortest day of winter

School is out
I'm on vacation

Five days until Christmas
We should have snow

And I find myself
Thinking of
a California sunset
and you.

About the Author

B arbara L. Eaton earned a Ph.D. in Shakespeare and Medieval Literature from the University of Maryland at College Park and taught at the college level for forty years. She chaired the Poets & Patrons of Chicagoland poetry contest and facilitated for the Illinois State Poetry Society. Barbara has published online and in various academic journals. She is named in *Who's Who in America*.